FOLLOW THAT DREAM
One Couple's Journey

THE STORY OF
Butch & Judy Farnum

BUTCH FARNUM

Follow That Dream: One Couple's Journey
by Butch Farnum

Copyright ©2021 Butch Farnum
All rights reserved

Published by
Partnership Publications, A Division of House To House Publications
Lititz, Pennsylvania 17543

ISBN: 978-0-9778614-6-0

Scripture quotations from The Authorized (King James) Version. Rights in the Authorized Version in the United Kingdom are vested in the Crown. Reproduced by permission of the Crown's patentee, Cambridge University Press

This book or parts thereof may not be reproduced in any form, without written permission of the author except as provided by the United States of America copyright law.

DEDICATION

This collection of stories is written for our children: Angela, Amy, Tripp, Erin, and Grace, who in so many ways have given these stories new life and meaning. Your mom and I are so delighted and blessed that the Lord gave each of you to us. We pray that your journey will be as rich and wonderful as ours has been. Center your life around Christ Jesus and He will give you the desires of your heart.

Love, Mom and Dad

CONTENTS

Foreword 9
Introduction 11

SECTION ONE: Childhood 13
1. Boyhood Memories 13
2. Crossing the Paved Road 15
3. The Ride of a Lifetime 18
4. Bat-killin' Time 20
5. Family Reunions 22
6. Three Rings 25
7. "You're Going to Burn the House Down!" 26
8. Beer Halls and Hunting Clubs 28
9. Boy Scouts and Ghost Stories 30
10. Our Gang 32

SECTION TWO: Teenage Years, Navy and Marriage . 35
11. Drunk and Disorderly 35
12. Brown-eyed Girl 37
13. "Hey Mom, I Joined the Navy!" 39
14. Newlyweds at Last 42
15. Alive by His 'Gace' 45
16. Report to the Chaplain's Office 48

Section Three: Bible College, Moving Home and Farming 48
17. Hippies and the Holy Ghost 49
18. Cows Across the River 53
19. The Desert will Bloom 56
20. Pepsi Cola Florida 59

21. Anywhere but There 61
22. Obedient but Struggling 64
23. Six Dollars and a U-Haul 65
24. Breaking the News—Again! 69

Section Four: Ministry and Bethel Church 71
25. Church in a Pick-up 71
26. Adopt a Child: World Premiere 74
27. Despise not Prophesying 77
28. Devil in a School Bus 81
29. Give Him Your Coat! 83
30. Is Everybody Gonna Leave? 86
31. Those are My Daddy's New Shoes 89
32. Second Fiddle 91
33. Fourth Generation Cotton Farmer 94
34. Judy's Dream Comes True 96
35. Courthouse Steps 98
36. One on One 101
37. Women in Ministry 103

Section Five: Family 105
38. Sunday Morning Rabbits 105
39. On the Coldest Winter Nights 107
40. Willing to be Wrong 112
41. Our God is Faithful 115
42. You're Not Listening to Me! 115
43. Out on Visitation 119
44. Deep Down Hurt and Anger 122
45. Fishing with Frank 124

46. Angel Called 126
47. Family Time 128

Section Six: Serving the Community 131
48. New Purpose..131
49. McMeeting 133
50. 'Phesians 136
51. Crack House Prayer 138
52. NBC Nightly News...140
53. Your Services No Longer Needed.........................143
54. Closed Chapters...146
55. Full Moon Birthday 149
56. "Dad, Look Around!" 150
57. Staying with Mickey..153
58. Trusted Stewards 155
59. Yellow Ribbons 157

Section Seven: Reflection and Transitions 159
60. Back to Her Roots 159
61. Parenting is Not for Cowards 164
62. They Can't Move!...167
63. The Phone Rang 170
64. One More Mountain 173
65. Another Closed Chapter 174
66. Miraculous Mud...178
67. Prophetic Promise 181
68. A Fitting Tribute to "Momma Judy".....................183

Epilogue 185

FOREWORD

Many of our Bible hero's lives were interrupted by an encounter with God. an angel, or any other vessel carrying His Word. At any time or place, day or night, God can speak to us. He might use life-changing visions, dreams or revelations of His will. God's powerful presence is but a moment away from us as it was for Noah, Abraham, Moses, Sarah and Mary the mother of Jesus.

Perhaps your life has been interrupted by a word from God, a dream or a vision. Like our heroes, we often struggle with God's call or message that resounds in the core of our being. It is no small thing for God to speak to us and redirect our lives. To some this becomes a message that haunts; for others, it brings great joy. For Judy and I, His will, has been the adventure of a lifetime and we "ain't done yet!" We hope that our story will in some way inspire you to follow that dream God has given you!

INTRODUCTION

To say that this book has been a "long time coming" is an understatement. We have been blessed to serve under the leadership of Butch and Judy Farnum for most of our adult lives. We have witnessed the Bible and the walk of faith we see in its pages, lived out before our eyes on a daily basis. We have watched as His Word has not only been preached from the pulpit but preached through the lives of these two precious people that have been gifted to the body of Christ for these generations.

It has been our pleasure to witness a good portion of what you are about to read in these pages. The stories and life lessons held within this book will encourage you, challenge you, and fill you with hope – the hope of our coming Jesus and the beautiful ministry of His servants in this day!

Although our precious Judy sees this long-awaited book come to fruition from the other side of Glory, she is very much a part of every word, on every page, and a continuing part of the ministry she and Butch built together that fills these pages.

Love you Papa and GanGan,
Joey and Renée

SECTION ONE
CHAPTER 1

Boyhood Memories

One of the few regrets I have in life is that I don't have a single picture of Sybie. Whenever I returned home after boot camp, I was always anxious to get to Sybie's house just across the field from our home place. While visiting her in that dimly-lit front room, I couldn't help but see the picture of me in my dress white uniform tucked along the edge of that old, framed mirror, amongst all her grandchildren, nephews and nieces. I was the only white kid in the bunch! Sybie was more than a mother to my two older sisters and me. She loved us and cared for us. We loved her during an era when there was so much divide between the races.

I grew up on a large plantation that had acres of virgin long-leaf pines and a large creek running through it. There was always a swimming hole, a swinging vine, my horse, and lots of fishing and hunting. I spent countless hours with my dad hunting quail, dove, fox, raccoon, deer and an occasional big cat on the home place and at various hunting clubs. You might say I had a Huck Finn boyhood. More than once I ran across the field to Sybie's house to escape a well-deserved whipping from my mom. Often, Mom would drive the old pickup down the field road to fetch me from Sybie. Usually, I would be hiding under Sybie's thick straw mattress while she pleaded my case with mother. It often ended with Mom promising not to whip me "this time" and

Sybie sending me home with a coke from her ice box and a slice of her wonderful sweetened bread she baked in her small wood stove. Funny, I believe I can still smell that straw mattress.

Sybie died before any of our children were born. Had she lived, their little faces would have been added to her mirror collection. Although I don't have a picture of my beloved Sybie to show my children, grandchildren or great-grandchildren, I can tell them stories and make our own wonderful memories with them.

CHAPTER 2

Crossing the Paved Road

Across the paved road from our house and Sybie's house were several sharecropper's houses. These families lived and worked on the farm. They were not employees. Instead, they worked a portion of the land owned by our family and shared a portion of their profit with my father, Captain Wes. One of those families had a boy, Hubert, who was the same age as me. Besides living on opposite sides of the paved road, we lived in two very different worlds. Being boys was the biggest thing we had in common.

I remember walking alongside Hubert as he plowed with the mule and helping him fetch wood for cooking and heating. One day I convinced Hubert to sneak off with me to the creek for a cool swim. We had a great time swinging out over the cold black water on a rope and splashing in it time after time. As we crossed back over the paved road, all cool and refreshed, we were met by his father. He was carrying a switch. I stood and watched as Hubert was switched by his father while being walked back to his unfinished chores. I'm quite certain that his father, John Wesley, would have liked to have used that switch on me too, but he only gave me a good scolding before sending me home.

I respected John Wesley before that day, but thereafter I judged him as being too hard on Hubert. After all, we were boys who just wanted to cool off on a hot summer day. John

Wesley seemed to be concerned with "little details" like Hubert drowning because he didn't know how to swim. In that creek you didn't have to swim, just stand up! Things being what they were, I thought it best not to try to convince him that there was no risk of Hubert drowning. I know that John Wesley spoke to my dad about the incident, but nothing was really said to me. A few days later, I crossed the paved road again and hung out with Hubert.

Both Hubert's dad and mine were victims of the times. Neither were perfect, but both wanted the best for their boys. We lived in a time of segregation. My father was born in 1896. We were divided by color, the past, public opinion and the paved road. We never talked about the swimming event going bad; we just played while I helped him with his chores. Little did I know about how my childhood with Sybie, Hubert and others would have such a profound effect on my life. I kept crossing that paved road and have continued to do so most of my life, not as an activist but simply as an expression of my heart that was formed on the Potter's wheel. Instead of being attracted by my childhood buddy, Hubert, I would have the Lord Himself beckoning me to cross on over.

The Bible tells the story of Peter crossing the paved road in Acts 11. While praying, Peter fell into a trance. He received a message from God about a new way of thinking about and responding to certain types of people. Peter's obedience to God's voice opened the door to many other opportunities to cross the paved road for God and see His mighty hand at work.

Our past is not always our enemy, especially when we obey God's unction and place our future into His loving hands.

"And I heard a voice saying unto me, 'Arise, Peter; slay and eat.' But I said, 'Not so, Lord: for nothing common or unclean hath at any time entered into my mouth.' But the voice answered me again from heaven, 'What God hath cleansed, that call not thou common.' And this was done three times: and all were drawn up again into heaven. And, behold, immediately there were three men already come unto the house where I was, sent from Caesarea unto me. And the Spirit bade me go with them, nothing doubting" (Acts 11:7-12).

CHAPTER 3

The Ride of a Lifetime

Another day—another adventure. I was riding my horse through the farm past Hubert's house towards the new interstate highway that was being built through the corner of our property. As I arrived at another sharecropper's house, their boys and I thought it would be a great idea to hitch my horse to their two-wheeled cart so we could all ride. It did not take us long to prepare the hitch and set off.

The two-rut road took us through some woods, opening out into the edge of one of the biggest fields on the property that bordered the soon to be I-26 highway. As we pulled up to the dirt embankment for the bridge that would cross over the "super slab," the idea of riding down the steep grade sounded like great fun. It only took a gentle slap on the rump with the reigns, and we were off.

The first sign of trouble was when Nellie's ears laid backwards as the cart ran into the back of her back legs. By the time we got to the bottom of the hill, she was stretched out in a dead run. The panic that Nellie felt was now upon the riders. The runaway scene only lasted a few minutes before my first passenger bailed. I can still see him tumbling down the sandy field road in a cloud of dust. We managed to make the turn through a cotton field where those who were working just stood in complete silence. One by one my buddies thought it better to hit the dirt instead of waiting for whatever lay ahead. All the "whooa"s in the world were not slowing Nellie down and as I rounded the corner of a neighboring farmer's yard, barely missing his milk cow, taking the pitcher pump out of the ground. Nellie ran under his shed and the axle of the cart brought the shed down on top of the cart. This finally brought Nellie to a halt.

My buddies had run off toward their own homes, and I was left alone with some explaining to do. This was one of the times I was referred to as "that boy of yours" by our angry neighbor. Daddy paid the bill, and we got what was left of the cart back to its owner. Probably more importantly, we all lived to tell the story! Just another day in the country with boys looking for adventure!

Little did I know at that age that my whole life would become an adventure. Some years would pass before my boyhood mischief would be turned into a lifelong mission. Like so many before me, I would follow Him, and He would make me a fisher of men.

"And Jesus, walking by the sea of Galilee, saw two brethren, Simon called Peter, and Andrew his brother, casting a net into the sea: for they were fishers. And he saith unto them, 'Follow me, and I will make you fishers of men.' And they straightway left their nets, and followed him" (Matthew 4:18-20).

CHAPTER 4

Bat-Killin' Time

We would sit on the front porch steps and wait. As soon as the first flight of bats would leave the attic peak, it was bat-killin' time! Well, I guess we should describe it as shooting-at-bats time, because even the best of wing shooters has trouble hitting a bat! Bat killin' was by no means limited to the front steps. Occasionally a bat would get into the house, usually in the front room at night. I am sure you have never heard such a carrying-on in your life! First, we had to close the doors to contain the bat, then get the broom or dust mop and knock it out of the air while ducking and diving. It was a loud event, probably a prerequisite to some new rock and roll dance steps. Those were good times in the country.

To be honest, I am not sure if the young fellows came over to our house to shoot bats or see my two older sisters. It was Carolyn, Georgia Ellen, then me. The guys would bring a guitar and the front porch would become a talent show. They were great guys except for the time they launched my newly-constructed raft off the top of the bridge. They laughed as it floated downstream in splinters. Caw Caw Creek ran through our home place and that made it the home of many a picnic and swimming party for folks from miles around. This was long before "No diving from bridge" or "No fishing from bridge" signs appeared. Folks used to sit on the bridge and fish by the light of a lantern without fear of being run over by some wild or thoughtless driver. We all learned to swim in that creek and learned to drive on that long dirt road that ran through the property.

Times were slower then and life in many ways was simpler. We were at home at night, where only select rooms were heated and lights were used sparingly. After family dinner, my sisters and I would wash the dishes and put everything away. Once the chores were done, we might watch a little television—one of the three channels available—before bed. Many refer to that time as the good ole days!

CHAPTER 5

Family Reunions

Family reunions on my mother's side were the best. The food was always great. We just couldn't wait for the first carload of cousins, aunts and uncles to arrive. After taking note of how we had all grown since the last time, we were ready to play, run and holler. That meant that we kids had to stay outside, out of earshot of the adults. The rule was that children should be seen and not heard.

The adult also had lively conversations. Mom's brothers were jokers and teasers. After a few beers they were in rare form and had so much fun telling stories on each other.

During one reunion, one of my cousins made it his mission to make life miserable for the chickens. No matter where they were, he had to chase them. He would run through the flock, laughing and hollering and waving his arms.

Back in those days, we children were usually warned once or maybe twice. If we persisted in doing whatever we were not supposed to be doing, we suffered the consequences. This time, after hearing all the ruckus from around the corner of the house and chickens running every which way, a stern warning was given: "You kids leave those chickens alone, before that rooster gets you!"

Well, that lasted only a few minutes and my cousin was back at it again. The flock had started to work its way across the two or three-acre front yard, but that boy couldn't help but make another run at them. All the sudden, we heard a scream. There he was, running towards the back yard wearing that rooster for a hat. He was crying and yelling for help. The rooster was pecking and spurring his head to beat the band. As he and the rooster rounded the corner of the house, the adults jumped up and started swatting the rooster off his head and shoulders. The rest of us kids were called down because we were hee-hawing about how funny he looked. It was a hoot! There was no serious injury done to the rooster or my cousin, but I doubt if he ever tried to mess with chickens again.

My sisters' husbands come from hard working, fun loving families also. At one of their reunions the story was told about how Uncle Barney's older brothers had convinced him that he could fly out of the second-story loft of the barn using his Papa's big black umbrella as a parachute. As soon as Barney jumped, the umbrella turned upward and down he went. Barney wasn't hurt, but the umbrella was trashed. After Barney's short flight was known and it was determined that he was not injured, what remained of the umbrella was used on the boys' backsides, including Barney's, to teach them a lesson. One might think that the impact of the landing would have been lesson enough, but Papa felt he needed to drive the point home!

Follow That Dream

I so hope that you and your families get together for food, fun and fellowship. There is so much in life to laugh about. Just be sure that the one whom the story is about can laugh, too! The Bible says, "a merry heart does good like a medicine" (Proverbs 17:22).

CHAPTER 6

The Three Rings

One of the fellows that frequented our home on the weekends worked for the telephone company. He gave me an old telephone bell that would ring every time it was plugged into an electrical outlet. We were the third party on a three party line so if the phone rang three times, that meant we had an incoming call.

Hiding behind the door by the outlet in the hall, I would wait until my sisters were busy, preferably outside. Then I would ring the bell three times. One of them would come running into the house to the phone in our parent's room, pick up the receiver and answer. Huh! "It must have been a wrong number," they would conclude.

I got by with that a few times until one day I couldn't hold back the laughter. You can only imagine how they reacted when they realized I was playing a practical joke.

My sisters and I never fought but we picked and prodded as normal kids do. Being the youngest, I always had a lot of adventures to share at the dinner table. Mother was often asked to "make Butchie shut up!" It's tough being the little brother, especially when both sisters belonged to the National Honor Society and I was completely disinterested in school! Georgia Ellen is now with Mom and Dad in heaven; only Caroline and I remain.

CHAPTER 7

"You're Going to Burn the House Down!"

Besides being haunted—according to my young mind—our home had many other unique features. The only heat or air we had was supplied by mother nature except for a wood heater in the living room and a wood stove in the kitchen. The Farnum house was a grand old home with many giant oak trees in the yard. Our house, like many of its era, was built with the kitchen separate from the main structure of the house. A large, screened porch or breezeway had been added to connect the two. I guess that added concern about the house catching fire.

As a boy, I was my father's constant companion. He fixed up a seat for me behind his seat on the tractor, and I would ride with him for hours on end as he broke ground for planting. I probably wasn't all that safe, but at least he knew where I was.

One day we were plowing a field adjoining the house when Mother suddenly appeared, waving her apron. We couldn't hear what she was trying to say, yet couldn't help but notice the kitchen curtains flaming up behind her. Daddy knocked the tractor out of gear, jumped down and crossed the field and fence in one motion. He was able to quickly put out the fire with no real damage. I guess the possibility of the house burning down was a reality in his mind.

On another occasion our first hot water heater was installed in the breezeway between the house and kitchen. Daddy had become very frustrated with the new gadget because the wind kept blowing the pilot light out. One day after being told that the pilot light needed to be lit again, Dad proceeded to tear the whole thing out and throw it out in the yard before it burned the house down! So, we were back to heating a big pot of bath water on the stove and toting it through no less than four doors between the kitchen to the bathroom. In the winter, the steam from the boiling water warmed the cast iron tub and the small bathroom.

One hot summer night, I was tired of sweating myself to sleep in my upstairs bedroom. I had found a small oscillating fan and was enjoying the cool breeze it produced. Laying there in my south seas island experience, I heard Daddy hollering from the bottom of the staircase. "Turn that thing off, you're going to burn the house down!" It would be a few years until I would know the world of controlled heat and air.

CHAPTER 8

Beer Halls and Hunting Clubs

Being my dad's constant companion meant I spent a lot of time in beer halls and hunting clubs. Dad and his buddies, "fair weather friends" as my uncle called them, drank beer and played gin rummy many days. During summer months I would sell catawba worms to the fisherman who stopped by for a cold beer. Winter months were spent at one of three or four hunting clubs.

As a small boy I would stay at the camp of the Rowesville Hunting Club instead of joining the deer drive with the others. Candy was an old black gentleman who cooked a wonderful lunch of fried chicken, sausage and rice. One Thursday morning Candy discovered he had not gotten enough lard to fry the chicken and sausage, so he sent me back to the small country town to fetch some. The old mule and I got along really good until we got to the edge of town. For some reason, the mule started going from one side of the road to the other wanting to stop at every house. The entire trip took me several hours.

When I arrived back at the camp, I asked Candy if that mule had ever acted that way with him. He laughed as he explained that he used that mule and wagon to pick up trash from those houses every week.

Back then mentoring was an unknown word to me, but I knew what it was to have fine old men like Candy to speak into my life and watch out for me while he fried some of the best chicken in the world over an open campfire. To me, Candy had the original recipe.

I spent many a night coon hunting with Dad and others. As a small boy I often got tired of trudging through the woods and swamps, so Daddy would take me back to the pickup to sleep while they tried for one more coon before calling it a night. That truck seat would feel so good as I pulled Daddy's old hunting coat over me. If it were today, I suppose Daddy could be charged with child endangerment. But back then he was taking care of me and raising me to live off the land: farming; hunting and fishing.

CHAPTER 9

Boy Scouts and Ghost Stories

My father had blessed two area Boy Scout troops with designated camp sites on the family property. One of those sites was in our pasture across the creek from our home. We had tons of fun camping, fishing and exploring the woods and fields. At night we would play hide go seek and sit around the campfire telling stories. One particular night when ghost stories were in rare form, I talked about our family ghost "Joseph" who lived in our house.

The story was that Joseph was a Torie who was hung in one of the giant live oaks in our front yard by the commander of the local militia. We were used to hearing strange noises during the night and my sister Georgia Ellen swore she saw Joseph at the top of the staircase one time. That is why I always ran up the stairs to my bedroom hoping Joseph wouldn't get me before I got the covers over my head!

After telling the Joseph story to my fellow Boy Scouts, we all went to our tents for the night. The three in my tent were aroused from their sleep by an unusual noise. Just enough time passed to get our imaginations racing before we heard a rub against our tent flap. So, with all eyes on the tent flap in the faint light of the dwindling campfire, a big grey head slowly protruded through the flap. I'm not sure if it was a yell or a scream, but two of us left out under the back of the tent, leaving the third scout standing his ground inside the tent, hatchet in hand. Outside, I was relieved to hear some familiar sounds and see our two grey horses running off into the night. Needless to say, it took some doing to convince the lone defender of our tent what had really happened.

Some years later, two of my teenage buddies were guests in our home. One was from out of state, so Billy, a master storyteller, and I had a good time priming Bob with Joseph stories before bedtime. Occasionally my mother would groan in her sleep, especially if she ate cucumbers or other such foods for dinner. Well, I guess the cucumbers were especially good that night because she let out a deep long groan to which my new buddy Bob sat straight up in bed and said, "What was that?" There was no way Bob was going to be convinced by Billy and me that Joseph wasn't prowling around, so Billy finally agreed to take Bob to a motel for the rest of the night.

Whether Joseph was real or not I don't know. But I do know he was the central character in a lot of funny family stories. Besides, we always had someone to blame things on!

CHAPTER 10

Our Gang

Frankie was my best buddy in the whole world. We played together for what seemed like forever at his house, my house, or his uncle's river house. Back then children were told to go outside and play. So, we spent a lot of time in the woods building camps and forts, walking logs across the creeks and occasionally finding the perfect vine to swing across accompanied by a Tarzan yell. We rode bikes all over creation.

As we got older, our mischief increased to include others. At night we would paint white stripes around an old nylon stocking filled with old newspaper and lay it on one side of the main road. From the other side of the road, we would hide in the ditch and pull this critter across the highway with fishing line in front of an unexpecting motorist. Traffic was sparse back then, but it was worth the wait. The bright lights (high beams) coming on meant we had their attention. If they stopped, we would dash into the dark of the woods, have a good laugh and set up the contraption for our next victim.

Our next best buddy was Howard. He lived about a mile from Frankie and about five miles from me on the same main road. My house was the last stop on the school bus route, so Howard, against his mom's instructions, rode the bus to my house. After a good snack we would go outside to find something to do. The tin roof on the old barn that had collapsed made a perfect slide except for the occasional head of a nail that was sticking up. We were having a great time until Howard was caught by one of those nails with his new dungarees that were meant for school. The terrifying sound of cloth ripping ended our play and we huddled together to concoct a believable story of how Howard's pants got ripped while he was where he was not supposed to be.

Howard would rather have faced a firing squad, but even so he called his mom to come pick him up. She was yelling over the phone about how he better be ready when she got there, and on and on. While she was swinging their old sedan around in our back yard, Howard was very careful not to expose his backside. But, as soon as he got in the back seat, she somehow saw his ripped pants. It was yell, yell, slap, slap, as she put the car in low gear. Down the driveway they went. It got even more intense when she missed the turn onto the highway and ran into the ditch while slapping at Howard. This had the makings of a rat-killin!

We didn't see Howard for several days, so it was up to us to carry on without him.

Another best buddy was Junior. Junior's farm was six or seven miles from my house. Being farm boys, we had a lot in common with the chores we were supposed to do. Besides, we both loved to camp. Junior's Dad had an old pickup that we would drive back and forth across their place and occasionally over to my house on the connecting dirt roads. One day after the return trip from my house to his, Junior's Dad said out of the blue, "Where's your coat?"

His Dad's face got red as a beet as he ordered Junior to get back over to my house and get that coat and come straight back. During the trip, we began to talk about the weather being great for a camp down by the pond. We could catch some fish and cook them for supper. At my house we loaded all the necessary camping equipment in the truck and made the return trip to Junior's house while refining our camping plans. His dad met us in the yard where we got out of the truck proclaiming our camping plans to which he barked, "So, where's your coat?"

Can you believe, we had gotten so excited about camping that we had forgotten the coat!

Years later, we would laugh about the crazy things we did as kids and marvel that we survived some of them. Today, I hear a lot of talk about it taking a whole village to raise a child. Back in my day, this was a reality. No matter who you were with or where you were, the adults would watch out for you, help train you, correct you and even discipline you if needed. And when you got home your parents already knew what happened and would reinforce what the other parent had done. It was great having that kind of childhood. To some degree, my kids enjoyed much of the same. I regret that for too many kids today, including my grandkids, the freedom of wide open spaces and watchful neighbors has been replaced with fences, gates and fear.

SECTION TWO
CHAPTER 11

Drunk and Disorderly

"Drunk and disorderly" sums up my early teenage years fairly well. I am not proud of that period in my life. Thankfully, the statute of limitations has exempted me from prosecution, and the prayers of my mother and others have kept me alive.

Years later, I met up with an old school chum and neighbor in a rather large law enforcement drug operation. As we did the man hug thing, he said, "Damn, who would have ever thought that I would be the police and you would be the preacher!"

I know I'm getting ahead of my story, but I want to remind you that a season in someone's life is not necessarily the summation of their life. People can change. This selection of stories certainly shows how one person was transformed and explains many of the characters and circumstances that brought it about. To God be the glory!

The journey of life for me has had many ups and downs. When I began to get sober, I remembered a vow I had made as a young boy standing between my arguing parents as I tried to get them to stop their frightening behavior. They continued arguing as I ran outside to the lot fence. Sitting on the top rail, I declared to the cows and horses through my tears that I would never drink and put my family through what I had just experienced. That vow would haunt me for some years because I failed to keep it. I was yet to meet the one who would hold me as I finally allowed God to break me free from that emotional stronghold.

"Of this I am confident, that he who has begun the good work in you will go on completing it until the day of Jesus Christ" (Philippians 1:6, MOFF). Often, God is at work long before we recognize it. There is no power that is not under His feet, including our past. He is Lord of all!

CHAPTER 12

Brown-eyed Girl

I quit the 9th grade before they failed me. One day I went by the high school with a buddy to see the fellows and a girl he knew. It turned out that this girl had a sister, a petite, brown-eyed Italian girl who really got my attention. My buddy and his date were going out that night and asked me if I would like to double date with her sister Judy. She was fifteen and I was seventeen. I met Judy's Mom and Dad that night and Mr. Charley gave me permission to date Judy on one condition: I had to attend church with her.

Church was not a big part of my life even though I came from a long line of ministers on my mother's side of the family. Like Jacob when asked to work seven years for a wife (Genesis 29), going to church was a small price to pay for being with Judy. She and her family would become the biggest factor in my coming to know the Lord.

I had quit almost everything in my life because it got hard or lost its luster, but I fell in love with this brown-eyed girl. We were from different worlds. I was a South Carolina country boy. In other words, a "red neck." She was a New Jersey city girl. My family ate butter beans, rice and gravy and biscuits. Her family ate pasta and sauce, bean soup and garlic bread. She was Pentecostal, I was Baptist. In many ways, it didn't make any sense for her father, at fifty years of age, to pull up stakes and move his family south. Surely the Lord had many reasons for their migration. Perhaps it was that Judy would befriend some of the first black students to integrate Orangeburg High School or that her mom and dad's Christian witness would touch so many in this community.

Even though I see the significance of those reasons and many more, I believe the Lord moved them to the south for me to fall in love with and make a lifelong commitment to Judy, my brown-eyed girl. We didn't have much of a chance by worldly standards, but God had a plan for our lives. I allowed her to see me cry and she became my safe place.

"Who can find a virtuous woman? For her price is far above rubies" (Proverbs 31:10).

CHAPTER 13

"Hey Mom, I Joined the Navy!"

I strategically made my way to my mother's dress shop on Main Street. Mom had managed dress shops in town for years and had built up a strong clientele because of the way she was a stickler about quality merchandise and customer satisfaction. Many of my boyhood afternoons were spent in town playing with my school friends. Before I could take off on my bike that we kept at the store, I often had to help straighten up merchandise racks and tables or walk the deposit to the bank down the street. The gang and I had lots of fun roaming the town and the beautiful blackwater Edisto River that runs through it. I later came to appreciate what Mother taught me about customer service and doing a job right.

Now, at seventeen, the bike was discarded and Mom's car was the ticket… if I could convince her that I really needed it. On this particular day, instead of the usual "I need to borrow the car," I had gone to break the news to her that I had joined the Navy. I was concerned that she would be upset because the Vietnam War was escalating and besides, I was her baby boy.

Mom's father and grandfather were preachers and she had two brothers in the ministry, but I had never known her to attend church. She was on the Methodist membership role and Dad was on the Baptist membership role. I was dropped off at the First Baptist Church many Sundays.

This day, as I entered the store, Mom was at her usual spot watching for incoming customers. I blurted it out: "Hey Mom, I just joined the Navy with two buddies of mine!" Instead of crying, she said, "Praise the Lord, somebody else is going to have to put up with you besides me!"

I was really shocked by her words, but she was right. I was the "problem child" in our family, nowhere near the scholars that my two older sisters Caroline and Georgia Ellen were. On final exam day for the ninth grade, I didn't even go to school. I hated school and did not want to endure another humiliating failure, so that day I drove Mom's car upstate to get a job on a cattle ranch that I had worked for when they brought bulls to the annual Orangeburg sale. Well, my plan did not really work out. The owners of the ranch were kind, served me lunch, and told me I should return to school. My letter asking for a job at King Ranch in Texas was given the same basic reply.

I had become a heavy drinker as a teenager, even though I had vowed as a boy never to allow alcohol to do to me what it did to my father and our home. Others already knew what I would eventually find out: I was unprepared for life. The Navy would play a big part in getting me ready for my future. This time my classroom would be the deck of a ship.

Stupidity, distance, and time could not separate me from the real love of my life. I wrote Judy a letter and told her that I loved her and asked her to forgive me for leaving her like I did. We continued to write letters back and forth. I soon mailed her a diamond and asked her to marry me. She said

One Couple's Journey

"Yes!" I came home on thirty days annual leave, and we were married. We had three hundred dollars and a borrowed car to use for our honeymoon. We spent one hundred fifty dollars to get towards the mountains and used the other one hundred fifty dollars to get back home.

Fifteen days after our wedding, I was back in the Philippines, waiting for my ship to port there. We wrote letters all the time. Sometimes I would get ten or twelve letters at once. I would line them up by the dates on the postmarks and begin to read them all. It was true in our case that "absence makes the heart grow fonder!" I would have given my right arm to be with Judy, but I still had things to learn about myself, life and the Lord. My drinking became heavier as my heart ached to be back home. Judy's picture was there at eye level when I would lie in my bunk, often with quiet tears in my eyes as I dreamt of when we would be together.

The Lord heard my cry and met me there. He began to rewrite my future.

"For I am persuaded, that neither death, nor life, nor angels, nor principalities, nor powers, nor things present, nor things to come, Nor height, nor depth, nor any other creature, shall be able to separate us from the love of God, which is in Christ Jesus our Lord" (Romans 8:38-39).

Being in the Navy was not the end of the world, and I was not alone!

CHAPTER 14

Newlyweds at Last

My first ship, the USS Henry W. Tucker (DD875), was ordered back to Long Beach, California after being home ported in Japan for several years. Judy and I had only been together about sixty days during our first two years of marriage. While in dry dock in Long Beach, we were able to create our first home together. During that time Judy was expecting our first child.

Several times the Tucker went to sea for a few days for "shakedown cruises." During one of those times Judy surprised me as she wore a maternity top she had sewn out of some leftover material from the curtains in our apartment. Like her sewing, there were a lot of things we didn't know about one another. Seeing her in that top gave me my first glimpse of her as a virtuous woman as described in Proverbs 31:10-24.

While in the Navy, during our first four years of marriage, Judy and I were only together for one year in Long Beach, California where our first daughter Angela was born. Complications in her pregnancy drew Judy back to her roots. She called the local Assemblies of God church for prayer, which led us to attend their service one Sunday night. I can't tell you what the pastor preached about, but to Judy's surprise, and mine too, I jumped up and ran to the altar call. I had no sooner returned to my seat than the pastor asked if "the young sailor who gave his heart to the Lord Jesus would like to come up and say a few words about what Jesus had done for him." Judy was in shock when I walked to the platform and began to talk about my encounter with Jesus that very night. Well, the truth is, that was the first of several times I went to the altar. Each time I reneged on part of my promise, but God never gave up on me.

A short time later Judy gave birth to a beautiful and healthy daughter. Judy's Mom risked her life by taking her first-ever flight to come and help Judy for two weeks and then we were on our own. I was so proud of Angela and was accused of pulling strangers off the street to show her off.

Several months passed. Angela, Judy and I needed more room than our no-bedroom apartment which was above a bus stop and across the street from a loud bar. Our search led us to a nice apartment in a residential section of town. We spent several days washing down walls, shampooing carpet, and doing a lot of heavy cleaning. We hired a van to move our few items of furniture while I was at work one day.

As I finished up the day and was about to leave the ship, I was handed new orders to another ship. It would take me back overseas. We did not even spend the first night in that apartment, and our few boxes and pieces of furniture went to storage. The landlord was so kind to not even give us our deposit back. I put Judy and Angela on a flight to South Carolina then drove the car across country, packed with the things she and Angela would need at home.

What seemed like a kick in the head at that time turned out to be God's provision for what lay ahead.

"But if you pray to God and seek the favor of the Almighty, and if you are pure and live with integrity, he will surely raise up and restore your happy home. And though you started with little, you will end with much" (Job 8:5-7, NLT).

CHAPTER 15

Alive – By His 'Gace'

On the single sheet of paper that the Australian sailor provided I wrote, "Dearest Judy, It is only by the gace of God that I am alive!" That was June of 1969. It would be three days before an accurate muster of the ship's company was made and almost a week before Judy and family would get any official news: 74 dead and 198 survivors. Until then I was missing and presumed dead by the local news reports.

Our ship was in a collision—cut in two by an Australian carrier. I don't have a word to describe the sound of the impact, but if you've ever been in a train wreck, it could be about the same. Anyway, upon impact, I woke up at some point during my brief flight from my bunk to the pile of shipmates and gear adrift on the deck. My first conscious moment was an eerie tomb-like silence. The next few minutes seemed like eternity as the ship made a hard roll to port before settling upright with a sharp list forward. Then all the hollering and cussing started. In total darkness and chaos, men scrambled to find cloths, battle lanterns and an answer. What in the world had happened?

Several days prior, my ship, the USS Frank E. Evans, had left her assigned duty in South Vietnam and joined an international exercise just outside the combat zone. My watch assignment as mount captain for the forward gun mount had been secured at midnight and now my very welcome night of sleep had been interrupted by what would be known as a naval nightmare. All those seemingly useless drills we had endured would now have merit; our training kicked in! Watertight integrity was set and we began to determine if we had sunk or were afloat. From below the main deck, we tapped on the fantail hatch and listened, determining that we were afloat. Taking my turn to escape through the opened scuttle, I knew something was terribly wrong when I looked up. Instead of the expected clear pre-dawn sky, there loomed the underside of an aircraft carrier flight deck! We had been cut in half by the Australian carrier, Melbourne!

Lots of stories could be told about those hours and days after the collision, but to me the most important one is that as I climbed aboard the Melbourne and an Australian sailor handed me that sheet of paper to write to my next of kin telling them I was alive and well. I wrote "Dearest Judy, It is by the gace of God that I am alive..." Yes, I was a half-baked Christian at best and I misspelled grace, but you don't have to spell it correctly to have it!

That letter is just one of many that Judy and I wrote to each other during those first years of marriage. I used this particular letter many times as I trained disaster responders all over the United States, especially with Christian groups. I am so thankful to be alive. Even so, I must live with the fact that so many others died.

One Couple's Journey

A young sailor from my home county died that day. He was the "good kid"—and I was not. Several years ago, God gave me the opportunity to speak at a memorial service in his honor at his home church. Family members and fellow survivors attended. I couldn't help but cry openly as I looked at all the nieces and nephews that never knew their Uncle Denny. I did not deserve God's blessing of a wonderful wife of forty-five years, five wonderful children, seven wonderful grandchildren and since that time a great grandson. Denny never had a chance to enjoy any of that. It makes me feel very sorry. This is another factor that takes my life purpose far beyond the usual measures of human success.

Mine is the story of two dreams. One is my own dream and the other is the dream of God's design. These two dreams could have clashed, but instead they have merged. It is like something old and something new coming together. In that process, the will of the Lord for our lives is realized. This new path takes us to wherever He will lead us. Our lives are not our own, but His. I did not realize it at the time of that naval disaster, but I was about to begin a new way of thinking and living.

"If ye then be risen with Christ, seek those things which are above, where Christ sitteth on the right hand of God. Set your affection on things above, not on things on the earth. For ye are dead, and your life is hid with Christ in God. When Christ, who is our life, shall appear, then shall ye also appear with him in glory" (Colossians 3:1-4).

CHAPTER 16

Report to the Chaplain's Office

Some hours had passed since the collision. Survivors had been transferred to the USS Kearsage. I was ordered to see the ship's Chaplain. In his office I was handed my Bible that had been recovered from the shipwreck along with a picture that was tucked between its pages. The Bible was mine, but the picture was of another shipmate's wife or girlfriend. The Chaplain seemed as puzzled about the picture as I was about where he reported my Bible to be found. That Bible had traveled halfway around the world with me and now it had apparently done some traveling of its own. It somehow had made its way into another compartment quite a distance from where I slept.

Some of the guys on the ship used to call me "Preacher" because I kept my Bible under my pillow. I greatly respected Judy's Mom and Dad who had given it to me before my first deployment. However, I was still living in my heathen ways at that time. The only time I would actually pick up the Bible would be when I was changing my bedding. A mystery still surrounds its travels during the collision and the following few minutes. As far as I know, only God knows what really happened, or perhaps a sailor who was facing the fear of death. God had mercy.

"But the Lord is faithful, who shall establish you, and keep you from evil" (2 Thessalonians 3:3).

SECTION THREE

CHAPTER 17

Hippies and the Holy Ghost

For the umpteenth time, Judy's sister Mary invited us to join her at the coffee house after our supper at the local fish camp. I deplored hippies because they protested the war from which I had almost not made it home alive. We finally gave in because Mary insisted that God was doing a marvelous work among the teenagers. They were getting saved and filled with the Holy Ghost!

To be honest, this Baptist boy had been to enough Pentecostal services with Judy and her parents to know that I didn't want God messing with me on Friday night after a long week on the farm. I reluctantly pulled up to the old city-owned river pavilion where white kids in Orangeburg had been congregating for decades, taking swimming lessons in their segregated swimming area on the Edisto River. For the past few years, the hippies were there to buy drugs in the small pine grove just down the hill from the pavilion. They were attracted to the music and the "party crowd" at the coffee house just a short walk away.

That night, the second story balcony was packed with jubilant kids, both black and white. Judy and I made our way through the crowd toward the music. There was Mary's husband Bob leading the "God Squad Singers" in a chorus about God telling Noah to build Him an "arky arky."

Follow That Dream

The last time I remembered being at the pavilion was when I was a teenager. I had gone for a dance. That time, I was drunk and decided to entertain people by turning a field mouse loose on the dance floor.

This night was different. We were quickly introduced to the adult couples from various denominational churches who seemed as pleased as peaches about what was happening. When the music broke, one of the kids talked about the joys of being saved. I was very afraid because I had been in this kind of environment before and had made some promises to God. One of those times was the Sunday evening service at Judy's Assemblies of God church where I found myself at the altar. Until that time, only God had kept His end of the bargain.

Back at the coffee house my heart was once again stirred. Once again, Judy would be shocked when several Sunday nights later I announced that I was voluntarily going to her home church. You guessed it, First Assemblies! The initial shock of me going by myself to her church was one thing, but when I came home at a late hour with a new-found friend, the Holy Spirit, she was totally blown away!

We soon became one among those who were as pleased as peaches at the coffee house as we witnessed a great outpouring of God's saving grace and life-changing power. Teenagers and young adults' lives were being transformed one after the other. Many of them were no longer going to the pine grove to buy drugs but were going there to gather up their friends and bring them to hear about Jesus at the coffee house. Revival had hit Orangeburg in the form of charismatic renewal. One would expect that all the parents of these young people and the local church leaders would be rejoicing, but that was not the case.

Someone once said, "The one thing we have learned from history is that we haven't learned anything from history!" Just as in the days of Jesus' earthly ministry, the established religious leaders, including many of the Pentecostals, had a problem with the new wine. Times have changed somewhat since the sixties. Some of those same churches that resisted the move of God then are currently allowing contemporary worship. Some have also cautiously crossed the racial barriers. In spite of their objections during that brief time in the sixties and early seventies, scores of young people were saved and launched into ministry for a lifetime, including me and Judy.

One of those teenagers was Cynthia aka "Bush" because of her bigger than life afro. God used her gentle spirit to help change one of the core values of my life and our ministry forever. As I drove into the yard late one afternoon, I couldn't help but notice two black children swinging. They were Bush's niece and nephew.

I went inside to be greeted by Bush. She had such a gentle sweet spirit much like my Sybie had. Although I never heard a demeaning remark concerning blacks in our home during my childhood, I had to acknowledge that the seed of racism was dormant in my heart. My uneasiness with these children playing in my yard told me that the

Navy Chief who had once accused me of being racist was right! That time years before, I thought we were just out drinking and having a good ol' time. Then this Navy Chief Petty Officer decided to blurt out, "Farnum, you're a racist!" I did not understand how I could be a racist and still eat and drink with him.

Up until that time, I had not been able to see it. Now that my life was in Christ Jesus, things and attitudes would be changed. "Therefore if any man be in Christ, he is a new creature: old things are passed away; behold, all things are become new" (2 Corinthians 5:17).

Years later a young church leader asked me in confidence, "What do you do when you're struggling with the black folks being in church with you?"

"Invite them over for dinner!" I replied. Like God did with me, I didn't give this young leader much choice, because God had a plan for our lives that included everyone being welcome in His kingdom and in His house and mine.

CHAPTER 18

Cows Across the River

I love the ways of cowboys, but being a cowboy in South Carolina is just not the same as what we see on the big screen. Nevertheless, I was determined to at least dress the part. One of the farms I managed had a herd of cattle pastured in the Congaree River Swamp. While moving the herd one day, two young heifers jumped in the swift waters of the Congaree and desperately swam for the opposite bank. Several days passed before I could line up two fellows with dogs and boats to help me retrieve the heifers. Danny showed up with his friend Dargen whom I had never met before. We loaded the dogs, ropes and other gear into the boats and across the river we went.

We tied the dogs onto willow branches far enough apart so they could not fight each other then went scouting the bank in our boat. We soon found one heifer dead in the willows downstream. We returned to the sandbar to begin our search for the other on foot. As we rounded the river bend, there were the two bull dogs reared up against one another in the shallow water of the sandbar. "Hurry," Danny shouted. "If we don't separate them soon, they will all kill each other."

I aimed the bow of the boat at the middle of the fury and gunned the throttle. Bang, boom, bump, bump and the two dogs emerged from the stern very bewildered as they looked at one another. Then Danny began hollering at me about killing his dog. Well, at least they were not fighting anymore!

After a quick medical check, we headed into the swamp. We sighted the heifer. The dogs caught her about a half mile from the boats. One rope was around the neck and another around one rear heel. That heifer had gone crazy by the time we pulled the dogs off her. All she wanted to do was fight us. So, one of us lit out for the sandbar with the heifer giving chase while another pulled back on the heel rope if she got to close to her target. Our plan was to get her in the water and make her swim back across the river, but all she wanted to do was fight. She managed to tag Dargen and scrub him in the sand before Danny and I could pull her off.

I know this is all hard to believe, because a small plane that flew overhead actually circled around for a second look. It seems they couldn't believe it, either.

After several failed attempts, our "Plan B" was to put the heifer in a boat and carry her across. We pulled her down and tied her up, but the six hundred-or-so pounds was too much for us to lift. We had to move to "Plan C." This involved taking the outboard and gear off my boat, laying the boat on top of the heifer, then flipping the whole shebang over. It worked. We were at last headed to the other side.

So here I was, crossing the Congaree River with a crazy 600-pound heifer tied up in a 14-foot aluminum jon boat with only two inches between the gunnel and the water. Our next challenge was getting the heifer out of the boat and up the four-foot-cut bank on the side of the river. We did it—and everyone lived!

Forty years later, I saw Dargen at lunch with a mutual friend. It took a few minutes to figure out who was who. When I realized that it was Dargen, we laughed and laughed as we remembered the sandbar rodeo with our young friend.

Maybe you didn't do crazy things in your youth, but I did. I was just thankful that we survived and could laugh about it later. The young friend I was with was amazed that these two old men had once been full of spit and vinegar.

Another commonality we shared with Dargen was our faith in Christ. Our crazy story was capped off with our thankfulness for faith and family. As we witnessed to each other, we witnessed to our young friend. In our own way, we both declared the witness of the psalmist David. "I have been young, and now am old; yet have I not seen the righteous forsaken, nor his seed begging bread. He is ever merciful, and lendeth; and his seed is blessed" (Psalm 37:24-26).

CHAPTER 19

The Desert will Bloom

Judy and I had been walking with the Lord for several years. Twice within a short period of time, I had a very profound dream in which the Lord told me that if I was willing to walk away from my life's plan and dreams of grandeur and follow His will, He would cause even the desert to bloom before me. In the dream I saw a dry sandy plot of ground with a beautiful rose growing out of it. That plot of ground was very real to me because it was a round exercise paddock on the farm that I managed. It was natural for me to lean against that fence railing and watch a high-strung thoroughbred run and buck off the edge.

In my dream, leaning against the same railing and looking at the same bare ground, there appeared a single rose bud. It took days of pondering and praying, but I was reminded every day of what God had shown me because that little exercise paddock was right in the center of my normal daily routine at the farm! Being a strong willed person, the Lord had to give me the same dream again some nights later. I am reminded of young Samuel going to Eli thinking that it was Eli who was calling his name in the night (1 Samuel 3:4-11). Yet in fact it was God.

Part of my struggle was trying to understand why God would choose me to do anything for Him. Years before I came to know Jesus, as a young man enlisted in the Navy,

One Couple's Journey

I remember staring into the dark one lonely night at sea in the Tonkin Gulf. I was wrestling with the reality of being unprepared for providing for my wife and child with only an eighth grade education. I had been a poor student all my life, but after being encouraged by some of my shipmates, I earned my General Educational Development (GED) as a high school equivalent diploma. After being discharged in from the Navy in 1969, a series of events led me to enroll in the local technical college where I earned an associate degree in agricultural technology. I was voted "Outstanding student" and awarded a place in Who's Who. Judy and I did all that while our family increased to three children, I took twenty-five credit hours per quarter and worked a full time farming job. No doubt, it was a God thing!

Upon graduation, I was recruited by a large farm cooperative as a local facility manager. The following year I was recruited back to my real love, a very diverse farming operation with cattle, horses and field crops. The challenge consisted of two farms that were almost in complete disrepair. The herd was neglected; the barns and fences were falling down. The crop land had been managed poorly and the equipment was in pieces. The equipment inventory showed that they had a combine, but I had not seen it under any of the sheds, so I asked one of the farm hands of its whereabouts. David scratched his head with the bill of his ball cap in deep thought and said, "Oh yea, it's up to the river farm where we finished up the soybeans last year!"

At some point earlier in my life I ignorantly declared how much I loved a challenge. Now I had a big one. David and I and several other hands rolled up our sleeves and went to work. Judy and the kids would come up fairly often and picnic under the pines at the farm where the horses were kept. I gave most of my time and energy to my first love, the farm. On Sundays after I had checked on the herd and the horses, we ministered in a local nursing home where I had my early experiences learning to teach God's Word. We also served in a local fellowship and coffee house ministry. We were too young to be tired and were thrilled to be serving God! I was fulfilled and living my lifelong dream: farming!

All my life had been about farming. The first field Daddy let me plant on my own is just a few miles from our current home. At sea, the ocean became a giant field to me. Australia had whispered of her adventure and opportunity, but now a new dream would consume my life.

In this dream the Lord gave me, I saw myself leaning against the paddock fence. The Lord said, "If you will give to me all of this you have loved and accomplished, I will cause even the desert to bloom before you." In my heart I gave it up but continued to faithfully work the farm for several years until the Lord closed that door.

"And it shall come to pass afterward, that I will pour out my spirit upon all flesh; and your sons and your daughters shall prophesy, your old men shall dream dreams, your young men shall see visions: And also upon the servants and upon the handmaids in those days will I pour out my spirit" (Joel 2:28-29).

CHAPTER 20

Pepsi Cola, Florida

Judy and I were married in 1967 while I was on annual Navy leave. Fifteen days after the wedding, I was back in southeast Asia and Judy was finishing up high school. My ship's home port was changed from Japan to Long Beach, California. As soon as we tied up in Long Beach, I hopped on a flight heading for home while some of my shipmates shopped for an apartment for us newlyweds. Judy and I piled our few possessions, wedding gifts mostly, into a '65 Falcon given to us by Judy's parents and set out for California in the dead of winter. I had never driven on ice or snow, but after our side trip to Indiana to pick up my best Navy buddy Dave, Judy and I were finally together in our first little apartment.

Ten years later, Judy and I would be taking another life-changing trip in the opposite direction. The Lord had spoken to us. The door to farming had closed. We were selling our newly remodeled home that we had bought from Judy's parents and loading up our four kids, dog and heading to Bible college. The children with great excitement told everyone we were moving to Pepsi Cola, Florida! Our two year old Erin stood on the car seat between Judy and I the entire trip not wanting to miss a thing.

Follow That Dream

We had met Brother Ken Sumrall at a service in South Carolina where he told us briefly about Liberty Bible College. Some family members and friends thought the Bible college just fifty miles from our hometown would be a more logical place for us, but because I believed in the manifestation of the gifts of the Holy Spirit, I wasn't welcome there. Six years earlier the Lord had spoken to Judy that we would be attending Bible college and now we knew which one.

In the face of many discouraging circumstances, we borrowed money against the sale of our home and headed out. Several couples from our home fellowship packed our U-Haul, followed us to Pensacola, unpacked us and returned to Orangeburg. You know, even strong willed people like me cannot accomplish everything by themselves. Judy and I have had so many dear people to encourage us and walk with us throughout our lives. We've even had a few to provoke us forward!

CHAPTER 21

Anywhere but There!

It's amazing what a couple of years in the right place will do for you! It was a struggle leaving our familiar world of family, friends and work, but this move turned out to be a very necessary preparation for our life's work. We didn't know it at the time, but our world view had to be changed. We had been in the right place that had become the wrong place. The once greatest fellowship and Bible teaching had turned into an agonizing time for us. God was saying something different to Judy and I that meant we would be misunderstood by our fellowship leadership. The once inseparable bond would become two ships sailing on different courses. For us, giving up houses and land was easy compared to giving up our spiritual father and mother and many of our wonderful brothers and sisters in the Lord. Our once soft nest was being transformed into a launching pad for our first solo flight.

All of this happened in the context of the early Charismatic Renewal when scores of young people and families were giving their lives to Jesus. Many of them were freed from the drug culture. Many traditional pastors, priests, church leaders and believers were also baptized in the Holy Spirit. Meetings like the Full Gospel Businessmen's Fellowship and others began to spring up with wonderful praise and worship where the gifts of the Spirit were flowing. Yes, there were some abuses in some of the streams, but the truth is the truth no matter who misuses it. In that context we made an independent decision to follow Jesus and His calling for us. We were offered monthly support so that we could return after graduation from Liberty Bible College to a staff position in our local fellowship, but the Lord spoke clearly to us not to accept it so we could be free to go anywhere He chose to send us.

I was able to give full attention to my studies at Liberty because of my G.I. benefits and some money we borrowed against personal assets. Judy was able to take some classes also, but her main objective was taking care of our four children and the home. Lifelong relationships had their beginnings at Liberty Church, Liberty Bible College and Liberty Christian School. Many other couples had pulled up stakes and made the migration to Liberty as we had. The stories were different, but the goal was the same: to follow Jesus! I can tell you now, merely singing the words "Where He leads me, I will follow" and literally doing it require a different level of faith and commitment.

Early into our time at Liberty the Lord led me to change my minor to pastoral ministries with a double minor in biblical counseling. He was setting us up for the biggest commitment yet. I was in my study one day when the Lord spoke to me again. He had already told me I would be a pastor even though others had prophesied differently. Now he was telling me that we would be going right back where we came from. I sat there in shock. "Lord you know..." I protested. I couldn't bring myself to tell Judy, but one night during the same period, while Judy was in the House of Prayer on campus, the Lord spoke into her spirit the word Bethel. Judy first though Bethel may be the name for a future child, so she tucked that away in her heart. God is in control! He had been preparing us for service in the place of His choosing, not ours. The dread was turned to excitement in both of us as the two revelations came together. Yes, we would have another child, but first we would give birth to a church called Bethel in our own hometown.

CHAPTER 22

Obedient but Struggling

Part of my struggle with returning to Orangeburg was that I did not want it to appear as if we were competing with our former fellowship group, even though we knew that the leadership there declared that the fellowship would never become a church. The founder of that group, like many in that season, had received what was described as the "left foot of fellowship" from his denomination because he had received the baptism of the Holy Spirit with the evidence of speaking in tongues. "And when the day of Pentecost was fully come, they were all with one accord in one place. And suddenly there came a sound from heaven as of a rushing mighty wind, and it filled all the house where they were sitting. And there appeared unto them cloven tongues like as of fire, and it sat upon each of them. And they were all filled with the Holy Ghost, and began to speak with other tongues, as the Spirit gave them utterance" (Acts 2:1-4, KJV)

Many Pentecostal and non-Pentecostal churches alike defrocked these men and women who became the pioneers of the Charismatic Renewal. Like those of the Azusa Street Revival in the early 1900s, both Catholic and Protestant believers revisited many truths from God's Word that had been explained away by the clergy or had been lost in the quest for acceptance in the mainstream of society. God was doing a new thing and we would have a substantial role in it. Only time and an open heart could clarify any misgivings.

CHAPTER 23

Six Dollars and a U-Haul

That check had never been late! There we were in Pensacola, being obedient to the word of the Lord, ready to travel back to Orangeburg with a total of six dollars in our pocket. Judy and the kids stood in the front yard of our rental house waiting on the mail man to bring our final G.I. Benefits check while the last few items were being loaded on the U-Haul truck. Those two years in Pensacola had been a time of new beginnings. We had invested about $60,000 in assets into this Liberty Bible College adventure. I was only nine hours short of my bachelor's degree in Theology. All the school bills were paid thanks to the sale of my motorcycle that a certain sailor just had to have. Pensacola was a place where we would have wanted to build three tabernacles and stay forever, but it was time to move on.

Going home this time was different because we didn't have a home to go home to. Judy's Dad was seriously looking for us a place because we planned to stay with him and Mrs. Mary until...

We had stayed in Pensacola to the last day of our rental agreement. Now, we could do nothing but stand and wait. It seemed the only thing moving that morning was the mail truck that drove right past our box without even slowing down!

Follow That Dream

Have you ever told someone what the Lord had said or tell four kids they are going home to see family and old friends and then not actually get going? "Oh Lord! What do we do now?" I cried. One couple who came to Liberty at the same time we did was standing there with us. They were just as broke as we were—but decided to loan us the money to get home. The Vincent's had been scraping for weeks, with children of their own, until some wages came in. The bank teller told Carl that his first paycheck in months hadn't cleared the bank yet, but I guess they could see the desperation on my face and handed Carl the needed cash.

We rushed back to Judy, his wife Phyllis, and the kids and were soon on the road! Our son Tripp, Natalie our dog and I were in the truck; Judy and the girls followed in the family sedan.

Twelve hours later we arrived safe and sound at Grandma and Grandpa Boyle's house. The next day we went house hunting, with Grandpa leading the charge. That afternoon we were informed of a house in town that was being vacated by a Christian couple, so we unloaded the U-Haul truck that had been parked in Grandpa's yard into this little house. Then the former tenant and I went to the landlord and introduced me as her new tenant. She was happy to have us, Grandpa was happy to have us just a few blocks away and we were all excited to see what God would do next.

One Couple's Journey

At Liberty we had lived in a nice four bedroom house. Now we were all packed into a six-roomed house with one small closet. Tripp shared a small room with the freezer and the bicycles; the three girls shared the dining room. The single bath off the hall was the busiest room in the house. This house had no heat nor air and at certain angles you could see a ray of sunlight through certain walls because it had no insulation either. But what could we expect for $125 a month? The winter cold was taken care of by a wood stove in the tiny hall and the summer heat was taken care of by several well-placed fans that we collected from Grandpa's attic. He just knew those old fans would come in handy one day and he certainly was right!

We would have four summers of memories from the Adden Street house. First and foremost, our fifth child Grace was born while living there. Secondly, we all laugh about the missionary from Africa who would stay with us only one night in the summer because it was too hot for him to sleep. And he was in the room with the freezer! During those dog days of summer, we judged the inside temperature by the long stem candle Judy had placed in the center of the kitchen table. When it melted over in the shape of a horseshoe, it was hot. Many evenings Judy straightened that candle back out and put it in the refrigerator for the next day.

One morning as Judy was walking from our bedroom to the kitchen to get Grace's bottle, she noticed tiny black specks all over the bottom of her white nightgown. It was a flea invasion!

Anaother memory from the Adden Street house is a word from the Lord, "Establish my house first and I will establish yours." As the word got around that we were back in Orangeburg, I was invited to a home to meet with a few couples that said they had been praying for the Lord to start a charismatic church. They thought I was to be the founding pastor. In June of 1979 we began to meet weekly to pray for God's direction. The Lord blessed those times of prayer and planning, and Bethel Fellowship Church was born. The Lord used seven families to start the first known interdenominational, interracial church in our area.

In September of 1979 we had our first public meeting in a rented hall. The Lord would not allow me to work any outside job during those months of prayer and preparation. He provided for us by having folks bring us groceries and offerings to sustain us. One day the kids were especially excited because someone delivered an old color TV to our house. It was the talk of the family, seeing everything in living color! Our bubble burst one evening when a visiting relative informed us that the TV was only showing in black and white. Now we knew why that family gifted us with a perfectly good color TV!

Again, the Psalmist David said, "I have been young, and now I am old; yet have I not seen the righteous forsaken, nor his seed begging bread" (Psalm 37:25). God is faithful.

CHAPTER 24

Breaking the News—Again!

It reached the point that my mother was afraid to open a greeting card from us because more often than not we were announcing the arrival of a new grandchild. It had become a family joke. The same was true when our fourth child, Erin, was born. It was soon discovered that fall was coming on and baby Erin didn't have any shoes. Judy and I didn't think about it during the warm months, but now we were wondering what would protect her tiny little feet from the cold. Judy's standard answer was, "The Lord will provide. He knows Erin will need shoes."

Grandma Mary got busy praying while Grandma Gertie got busy buying a pair of shoes for Erin. And by the end of the week, Erin, who couldn't even walk yet, had ten pairs of shoes in the closet!

Both of our families were always very generous towards our kids. They may not have understood everything we believed or did, but they supported us and loved us. God provided for us time and time again. By His hand we were able to raise all our children to adulthood without any health insurance. The one time we did buy some health insurance, everybody got sick. So we canceled the coverage. I am not intending to condemn health insurance. I am just giving a testimony about God's provision for us.

At times, God would provide through some unusual avenues. After all, it was His idea to "supply all our needs according to His riches in glory" (Philippians 4:19). We just trusted Him and were obedient to what He put in our hearts to do.

Don't delay your obedience just because the books don't balance. If we had waited until conventional wisdom said it was alright, we would have missed one of the greatest treasures of our lives: our children, their children and their children's children!

SECTION FOUR
CHAPTER 25

Church in a Pick-up

Every Sunday morning Mr. Charley (Grandpa), Tripp and I would load all the church equipment from our bedroom into an old Datsun pickup I had acquired from a Baptist deacon and head towards whatever building we had been able to rent for that day's service. Because Tripp had the freezer and bicycles in his room, it was only right that Judy, Grace and I had the church equipment in ours! We did not have a permanent church home at that time, so we rented various buildings around the city. Sometimes we didn't know where we would meet the next Sunday, but the Lord would provide, and the saints would spread the word about where to gather.

On more than one occasion, Tripp, Mr. Charley and I had to sweep beer bottles out from the previous night and spray tons of air freshener as we pled the blood of Jesus over the place we were meeting. The main reason we couldn't rent the nicer places or the school buildings in town was that we were an interracial church. So, God met with us in pool halls, beer halls, fish camps and fraternity halls. The owners of one hall that we rented most often used the proceeds to renovate the building. This worked well for both our interest. However, once they finished their projects list, they told us that we could no longer rent the facility. I think they had found greener pastures.

Follow That Dream

There was at the time a fine old two-story brick home for sale that would make a good starter building for Bethel, but we needed $25,000 up front to close the deal. The Lord had brought a couple into our lives that gave us the needed cash out of the equity they had invested in a lake house they were selling. Isn't God amazing? The residential neighbors were alarmed about the potential noise, parking concerns, and just the idea of having a church in the neighborhood. They tried to block the sale, but the Lord prevailed. We immediately set out to calm their fears about having a religious cult in their neighborhood. I guess a Lutheran Church and a Jewish Synagogue were enough for them already.

Most of the renovations on this our new church home were done in the evenings and on Saturdays. One Saturday I was alarmed by how much noise the kids, about twenty of them, were making outside. As I looked through a front window facing a heavily-traveled street, I saw these kids chasing each other in a single file line with white dust masks on their heads for hats. Thinking of it now is a lot funnier that it was at the time. But stuff happens, and we had better learn to laugh through it.

It wasn't long before we had two services on Sunday mornings. The early service had a lot of denominational members who wanted to get in on the praise and worship before they attended their own churches. God was faithful and His people were too!

One Couple's Journey

"All the believers were united in heart and mind. And they felt that what they owned was not their own, so they shared everything they had. The apostles testified powerfully to the resurrection of the Lord Jesus, and God's great blessing was upon them all. There were no needy people among them because those who owned land or houses would sell them and bring the money to the apostles to give to those in need" (Acts 4:32-35, NLT).

CHAPTER 26

Adopt a Child: World Premiere

We sat around the kitchen table one Saturday evening putting together adoption packets with Mack and Peggy. This would be the second world premiere for Judy and me. The first was when we received free tickets to a movie at Grumman's Theater in Hollywood with all its glitter and glamor while I was in the Navy. Big-name stars dotted the audience and the camera flashes were endless.

This second premiere wasn't about making anybody richer or more famous. It was about feeding and giving medical and dental care to orphaned children in a distant land. There was no fanfare here in our little rental home.

Mack and Peggy had been our friends from our time at Liberty Bible College. They were retired from a successful business career and relished their grandchildren. Instead of kicking back and enjoying their golden years here in the United States, they had a vision to become missionaries to an impoverished and rebel-infested area of Guatemala. Back then, fifteen dollars a month was a lot of money for us because we were just starting a new church and living on faith with five children of our own to raise. I have learned, however, that human reasoning will often be in conflict with faith. Many had already questioned our decision to cash in our assets and go to Bible College. "Why not wait?" they would ask. "What about your children?" "Aren't you afraid?" They had their lives and priorities and we had ours. We were to follow Jesus and trust Him every step of the journey!

As we sponsored a child in Guatemala, we were setting an example of faith for our family and young church. It was a great opportunity. Our children were excited to know they had a little adopted sister in Guatemala. Everyone was willing to sacrifice a little to share with Sonia.

After the Sunday morning service Judy and I shared the excitement with Mack and Peggy over the number of children that were adopted. The believers at Bethel were seeing beyond the walls of the church and catching a vision for world missions and the great commission.

"And he said to them, 'Go to all the world and preach the gospel to every creature: he who believes and is baptized shall be saved, but he who will not believe shall be condemned. And for those who believe, these miracles will follow: they will cast out daemons in my name, they will talk in foreign tongues, they will handle serpents, and if they drink any deadly poison, it will not hurt them; they will lay hands on the sick and make them well.' Then after speaking to them the Lord Jesus was taken up to heaven and sat down at the right hand of God, while they went out and preached everywhere, the Lord working with them and confirming the word by the miracles that endorsed it" (Mark 16:15-20, MOFF).

Some years later my trip to Guatemala included the graduation of our little girl from the Adopt-A-Child program. Sonia had grown into a lovely young lady who had not only been fed good nutritious food but had been rooted and grounded in the Word of God. Mack and Peggy legally adopted a Guatemalan boy. As a young man, he came to the states, became a physician and returned to his native country to serve his people. When Mack died, his wish was to be buried in the land that he loved, Guatemala. What a commitment!

All of us have been challenged sometime or another by people like Mack and Peggy. We don't have to be just like them, but we do need to be true to our calling. Jesus said, "I tell you truly, no one has left home or brothers or sisters or mother or father or children or lands for my sake and for the sake of the gospel, who does not get a hundred times as much—in this present world homes, brothers, sisters, mothers, children, and lands, together with persecutions, and in the world to come life eternal" (Mark 10:28-30, MOFF). To do any less is to miss the adventure of a lifetime and the personal fulfillment that can only be found in obedience to Jesus.

CHAPTER 27

Despise Not Prophesyings

"Rejoice evermore. Pray without ceasing. In every thing give thanks: for this is the will of God in Christ Jesus concerning you. Quench not the Spirit. Despise not prophesyings. Prove all things; hold fast that which is good. Abstain from all appearance of evil" (1 Thessalonians 5:16-22).

Jesus came with a "now" Word, a rhema Word, that was met with great skepticism and debate from the religious leaders of His day. The same situation exists today. Organized religion has chosen to dispensationalize and reason away portions of the Bible to suit its personal belief systems. For us as a family, the voice of the prophets has had great impact on our lives and ministry.

As a young pastor at a conference in Tennessee, Dr. Bill Hamon called Judy and I and our four children out of the audience to come to the front. He wanted to prophesy over us. As Dr. Hamon began to pray, he stopped and said, "There's one more. Why is the Lord showing me that there is one more?" Our three-month-old baby girl was in the nursery. So, the service was stopped until Grace was brought into the auditorium.

Then Dr. Hamon began to go down the Farnum family line and prophesy over every member. Judy and I gained great insight into the lives of our children that day. To this day, the Word of the Lord has proved to be very accurate. Jesus often told His followers, as recorded in Matthew, "He who has an ear, let him listen to this" (Matthew 11:15, MOFF). We were wise to listen.

"You will be a community man, going about doing good, doing good" was what Dr. Hamon spoke over me. Many pastors are discouraged by their congregations or church leaders from using their time to minister outside the four walls of the church. That was not the case with Bethel Church. However, I had been battling inside myself with that desire to be involved with extra local ministries. There had been an imaginary wall between "the norm" and what the Lord had been speaking to me and the doors He had opened. It was not just about the prophecy giving us direction. In this case, it was a strong confirmation of how the Lord was leading us.

We have one prophet who has ministered at Bethel annually for the past thirty five years. Despise not prophesying! What was prophesied over us almost thirty-five years ago is clearly seen today. If we had not embraced the word of the prophet, our impact on our community would have been limited to those we could bring inside the walls of the church. Our community involvement began years before the term "marketplace ministry" was coined.

The mayor of our city was a regular at our monthly Ministers' Fellowship. He once shared with us a vision of having a nativity scene in the city-owned Edisto Gardens at Christmas. We were all supportive of his desire and collected enough funds to more than pay for the project. Because I was the founder and convener of that fellowship, I made the first pledge toward the mayor's vision. Today, the entire garden is filled with elaborate Christmas lights and displays, including a new nativity scene! Very few people remember the humble beginnings of that project, but that is okay because the most important thing was our faithfulness to who we are in Christ.

That same mayor asked for our assistance in establishing an annual Mayor's Prayer Breakfast which is still going on today. Sadly, during that same period, a city police officer was killed in the line of duty resulting in the formation of a group called Citizens Against Crime. Somehow, I was the only pastor included in the leadership of that group.

After this tragic event, a small contingency of police chaplains from coastal South Carolina came to Orangeburg to give support to the department and the victim's family. They were such a great asset to the community that the question arose, "Why can't we have our own chaplains to serve our city and county departments?" All eyes turned to me as that question was being asked. I had some hospital chaplaincy experience but knew nothing about serving the city and county officers.

Before I could protest, I was nominated to take this role. I enlisted the help of the law enforcement advisor on the committee, and we got started. Two years of research, development and intensive training produced four brand new volunteer chaplains for service.

The list could go on of the ways one small church got involved with community leaders in meeting many needs. For me, it all started when fivefold ministers in the church laid hands on me and faithfully taught me the Word of God.

"And he gave some, apostles; and some, prophets; and some, evangelists; and some, pastors and teachers; For the perfecting of the saints, for the work of the ministry, for the edifying of the body of Christ" (Ephesians 4:11-12).

"Study to shew thyself approved unto God, a workman that needeth not to be ashamed, rightly dividing the word of truth" (2 Timothy 2:15).

CHAPTER 28

The Devil in a School Bus

As I drove into the parking lot, I noticed small clusters of teenagers sitting or lying on the grassy areas surrounding the Emergency Room entrance. I slowly walked toward a group of three adults. I could hear many of the teens crying; they looked almost terrified. The ladies were cordial, but it was obvious that they would rather have had a doctor talking to them than a local pastor.

I had been called by a lady in our church who found out that two busloads of band members who were traveling through our area had arrived at the local emergency room, suffering from food poisoning. As I confirmed the story with the three chaperones, I thought it odd that the two buses had stopped for lunch at different restaurants and yet all the travelers had food poisoning. I once again turned my attention on the teens. I overheard one girl say to her friends, "I told him he'd better stop because he was scaring me."

I crouched down by the girl and introduced myself. I asked her what it was that scared her. She told me that one of the boys had a crystal ball in the back of one bus and had been holding a seance attempting to communicate with the devil. The evidence indicated this young fellow somehow managed to dial the right number because not only were these kids really frightened, but others among them were being treated in the emergency room for vomiting, emotional distress, and other ailments.

As I entered the second bus, I was greeted by a tangible heaviness. A voice from the back row seat said, "I know who you are!" I introduced myself as a servant of the Lord Jesus Christ and he spoke back declaring himself to be a warlock.

"It doesn't matter to me what you are or who you think you are, you are to stop whatever you are doing to frighten these kids now! Your time is up and your power over them is broken in Jesus' name!" I remember being amazed that the whole confrontation lasted only a few seconds and the victory was won. As I exited the bus, all eyes were glued on me. I told the kids who witnessed our brief exchange not to worry because everything would be fine for the remainder of their trip. I then reported to the three chaperones what I had discovered.

I am not sure that they had any idea what I was talking about, but they thanked me as I assured them the rest of their trip would be peaceful. I drove away thanking Jesus once again that His Word was true, and He has given us power over all the power of the enemy. "Then he called his twelve disciples together, and gave them power and authority over all devils, and to cure diseases. And he sent them to preach the kingdom of God, and to heal the sick" (Luke 9:1-2).

CHAPTER 29

Give Him Your Coat!

We were once again being blessed of the Lord by someone He sent our way. A young pastor from Africa was recommended to us by a dear friend and mentor. He greatly blessed our church gathering on Sunday. While he was staying in our home, we noticed that the pastor had no coat. It wasn't all that cold, but he was accustomed to the hot, arid climate of his homeland, so he was definitely feeling cold.

As I pondered this situation and begin to think where I could get him a coat, the Lord said to me, "Give him your coat!" After further reasoning, I slipped away to my closet where my two coats were hanging. Based on my own reasoning, I reached for the army field jacket only to be admonished by the Lord that I should give him the other coat.

"Well, I'm sure he would be happy with any coat that would keep him warm" I protested. "Lord. you know how much I love this coat and how I planned and saved to get it." This coat was a part of my identity. It represented my dream as a young man to be a cattleman.

"Yes, I know, and I want you to give it to him," I sensed God was saying in response.

Follow That Dream

I reluctantly removed my prize coat from the closet, hanger and all, and gave it to our guest pastor. Oh! He was elated over that coat, and I was contemplating the lesson the Lord was teaching me. It was a follow-up lesson to "obedience is better than sacrifice, to harken is better than the fat of rams" (1Samuel 15:22).

This encounter took place during my early development as a pastor. I had read these passages and maybe even preached from them already, but now my Lord was giving me another very practical lesson on obedience and sacrificial giving. David declared he would not give anything unto the Lord that did not cost him anything! (2 Samuel 24:24). Here I was, wanting to give a coat that had been given to me instead of giving the one that had cost me dearly.

No matter what our giving record has been, the Lord will give us opportunities from time to time to renew our obedience to His voice and open new doors of blessings. I've never had another coat like that one, but Judy and I have been given countless blessings by the Lord and His servants.

This leads me to ask: when is the last time you had a conversation with the Lord? Do you immediately recognize His voice? Any conversation with Him, even correction, is wonderful because the Father loves us and has our best interest at heart.

"Truly, truly I tell you, he who does not enter the sheepfold by the gate but climbs up somewhere else, he is a thief and a robber; he who enters by the gate is the shepherd of the sheep. The gatekeeper opens the gate for him, and the sheep listen to his voice; he calls his sheep by name and leads them out. When he has brought all his sheep outside, he goes in front of them, and the sheep follow him because they know his voice" (John 10:1-4, MOFF).

CHAPTER 30

Is Everybody Gonna Leave?

Our oldest daughter Angela sang "The Warrior is a Child" as a teenager. The title tells it all. Like Elijah's intense battle with the prophets of Baal, we often find ourselves depleted of all strength of soul and body.

It had been a long disappointing day and I was so discouraged. I needed some reassurance, so I drove over to see Scott at the nearby tennis courts. I called him off the court and we sat on my pickup tailgate. "Is everybody gonna to leave?" I asked. Scott replied that he had no plans to go anywhere and in his last conversation with the Lord, He wasn't leaving Bethel either.

No matter what the presenting issue is, (I think Judy and I have had them all), it always feels like abandonment and personal failure when you are a small church pastor and things go wrong. If for no other reason, your life becomes so intertwined with the church members. If we are not careful, we cross the line and become dependent on people instead of the Lord.

We have so many stories about the various times of exodus of God's people from our lives and ministry. Though a few gave us a sigh of relief, many departures were accompanied with pain, feelings of failure and a deep sense of loss. But God never let us stay discouraged, He always gave us encouragement! For instance, on a landmark celebration of Bethel, "Ten Years Old and Growing" was our theme. There were tee shirts, a big banquet with the mayor present and great accolades. Bethel was always a marketplace church. We had led or supported many community projects. I was also involved in other local ministries. All of that gave great opportunities for church members to be church ministers.

Judy and I were happy to see the church celebrate the Lord and His victories, but we never desired to be the center of attention. We were happy to see that the church that started out with one black couple out of seven families had grown to be a congregation of with about 60% black members. We had blacks in key leadership positions at Bethel in a community that was also known for the Orangeburg Massacre. One couple in particular, both educators, were greatly loved and admired. Clarence and Tresmaine brought so much life and godly character to Bethel and the community. I was sure that the Lord had sent me my co-pastor. God had blessed us with a new facility and great ministry team.

Our September triumph was turned into mourning shortly after Christmas when several influential couples left the church. Even though they had good "we feel led" and "God is speaking to us" exit speeches, we knew that the ugly head of racial prejudice had raised itself again. This attack of the enemy would be costly in momentum as well as finances. We all paid a common price to be at Bethel, the white members were marked as "those who went to church with black folks" and the black members were branded as "those that went to that white church." Please forgive me for distinguishing our members based on skin color. I do so only to describe the situation. I know that in Christ there is neither Jew nor Greek, black nor white, but I also know that going to church and being in Christ are two different things.

Orangeburg today is almost the same as it was back in 1989 when this happened. The community is still racially divided, especially on Sunday mornings. Just before the end of that very difficult year another church elder and his wife came by our home to give us a tithe check. We chatted and I placed the folded check on the centerpiece of the kitchen table. A few days went by and the elder called and asked if I had deposited that check. I replied "no" and replied "no" again when asked if I had looked at it.

I went home and looked at the check. I immediately called Judy to ask, "Do you know the amount of that check on the table?" She also said that she had not looked at it. "It is twenty-five thousand dollars," I exclaimed. It wasn't all about the amount of money. We were feeling rejected and forsaken. This check reminded us once again of our Heavenly Father's care and faithfulness. We must never forget that the Lord has a reputation of providing for those who journey with Him!

"And Elijah the Tishbite, who was of the inhabitants of Gilead, said unto Ahab, As the Lord God of Israel liveth, before whom I stand, there shall not be dew nor rain these years, but according to my word. And the word of the Lord came unto him, saying, Get thee hence, and turn thee eastward, and hide thyself by the brook Cherith, that is before Jordan. And it shall be, that thou shalt drink of the brook; and I have commanded the ravens to feed thee there" (1 Kings 17:1-4). Thank God for His ravens!

CHAPTER 31

Those are My Daddy's New Shoes!

It was a beautiful afternoon for a church picnic. The host family lived on a large farm with plenty of room for games and a large pool which became the center attraction. Most of the adults were sitting around the pool watching the kids having a great time swimming and playing water games. As the afternoon slipped away, some of the church leaders started throwing one another in the pool. As they searched the horizon for a new "victim," their eyes landed on none other than their pastor.

I had been watching this conspiracy out of the corner of my eye and was determined to take it like a sport. That meant I would put up a good fight. After just a short struggle, I found myself being heaved upon the shoulders of four "church leaders" who were headed toward the crowded pool. I managed to get my wallet and watch safely on dry ground before I was airborne. Then came the big splash. I was down in the water.

As I laughingly climbed out of the pool, my slacks and sport shirt drenched, my daughter Erin shouted out, with as much indignation as she could muster, "those are my Daddy's new shoes!" So they were. Small church pastors are generally not known for having an abundance of new shoes, nor expensive shoes. I think those shoes shrank two sizes before they dried out. But what didn't shrink was my example within the church body, especially the leadership team. It is worth a new pair of shoes every now and then to be seen as a normal human, to enjoy clean fun and be one of the guys. It's important to have fun with your Christian brothers and sisters – so lighten up!

CHAPTER 32

Second Fiddles

Standing beside every successful church leader, business leader, or political leader are faithful men and women who carry out the daily task of supporting that key person. Like in music, the rhythm section supports the lead instrument. I am told that the rhythm section can stand alone, but the lead cannot. Any leader who thinks they can do things all by himself or herself is foolish and will soon suffer his or her own undoing.

As young believers, Judy and I were blessed to have mentors who allowed us to be "hands on" in ministry. Information alone does not equip the saints for the work of the ministry. Jesus' pattern was to teach, demonstrate, give authority and open opportunities. That example became a key principle of our ministry. God established faithful men and women around us to keep the rhythm of the ministry going forward as we led. This has been true for every ministry endeavor, especially at Bethel.

One dear person protected the integrity of the ministry for our entire twenty-seven year tenure. Earle was our church treasurer. He did such a superb job that our finances were always received and handled in a professional and godly manner. He was also a trusted friend. He used his gifts and talents to wholeheartedly support the vision of the house. Earl's ministry gifts allowed Judy and I to be free from handling finances and trying to keep track of who gave what. That, dear friend, is a great blessing!

Many others took charge of various aspects of the ministry just like Earle did the finances. In an orchestra, the second fiddle fills in the musical score that the first fiddle leads; together they make a harmonious sound. "Second fiddle" in any organization is a trusted position to hold. Being in that position allows you to lift the hands of others. In leadership there are always weaknesses that need to be supplemented with the strength of others. This support could include warning the primary leader about any blind spots that he or she does not notice.

One day I realized that as much as the Lord was using me to build His church, He was also using the congregation to build me as a pastor. The two work hand and hand. There is no place for the idea of a "big me" and "little you." Though we may have different positions and different levels of responsibility, we are called to the same calling, "the work of the ministry." The relationship between Moses, Caleb and Joshua gives us a powerful example of the type of servant leaders God used to deliver His people from bondage and lead them to the promised land.

Every person who comes to Christ needs others with a willing heart to travel with them on their journey from one lifestyle to another. All of this begins with a servant heart. I have watched and felt the sting of a few overly-ambitious people through the years. Some of these could even be ambitious for their spouse, trying to gain a sense of power through them. It is part of our human nature to sit by the side of a recognized leader as a way of gaining stature or superiority. However, spiritually speaking, our calling makes a place for us. Promotion is from the Lord.

I was listening to a younger pastor one day who was telling me all the things he intended to do in our community in a somewhat arrogant way. I said, "So, you believe you are supposed to be the apostle over this area?" His was quick to answer, "Yes!" He was not content with the situation he was in, yet he had resorted to campaigning and conniving strategies instead of being faithful in the little things and allowing the Lord to place this leadership mantle on him. Unfortunately, his tenure was short because people began to see his agenda. He was using that pastorate as a stepping-stone to greater things.

In the Kingdom of God, promotion comes from the Lord. The place of others in the promotion process is to recognize and confirm as the Holy Spirit directs. Our part is to remain humble and serve with a sincere heart wherever God has placed us. We are to use the gifts and talents He has given us for His glory. More of these truths can be found in Romans 12 and 1 Corinthians 12.

CHAPTER 33

Fourth Generation Cotton Farmer

Years had passed since that night in the Philippines when a Navy Chief called me a racist. At the time, it shocked me. I was now pastoring an interracial church in the deep south. As I previously stated, God started a work in me during the coffeehouse days. I thought it was finished, but the Lord could see more work to be done. A Servants Conference flier from Bishop John Meares' church in Washington, D.C. came in the mail. It looked interesting, so I traveled to D.C. to attend the conference.

While there, I was greatly intrigued by this large inner-city church: a predominately black congregation led by a white pastor. I was also very impressed with the servant spirit that was exhibited during the entire conference. In one of the evening services, I found myself being drawn, almost transported, to the altar. All I can tell you is that God broke something deep inside of me concerning my preparation to serve Him in the place He had planted me.

I later received a church newsletter containing a photo of an altar call from this Servants Conference. Guess who stood out. There I was, a fourth generation cotton farmer, the only white pastor from below the Mason Dixon line. God changed my heart at that altar.

"Search me, O God, and know my heart: try me, and know my thoughts: And see if there be any wicked way in me and lead me in the way everlasting" (Psalm 139:23-24).

We all have a past that is contrary to God's Word and His desire for us. We must not allow our pride, prejudice or anything else hold us back from doing His will. What we resist today could be the very key that opens tomorrow's door!

CHAPTER 34

Judy's Dream Comes True

It had been a while since Cal and Bu moved to Switzerland to join YWAM. Out of the blue, Cal called one day and said he wanted Judy and I to come to Lausanne and lead a missionary training school for a week. Missionaries from Europe and Africa and some local YWAM staff would be there. Many of them were battle weary. The second week we would tour the country with Cal and Bu.

When I told Judy the exciting news, she immediately began to tell me all the reasons why she could not go. Several days passed before I called Cal and told him that Judy felt like I would have to come alone. Cal quickly replied, "If Judy doesn't come, you should not come, either!" That was the answer we needed.

Wow! The Lord was taking us to Switzerland! But it was hard for us to understand why the Lord would want us in Switzerland. There were so many other well known Bible teachers, speakers and counselors. Besides being with our dear friends, what else did we have to offer? Could it be that the Father knew of a little girl's dream to one day visit the homeland of her childhood friend, Cornelia? Cornelia had told Judy stories about the beautiful country she came from; Judy had longed since that time to see it for herself one day.

Before long, it was time for our departure. Judy's Mom and Dad took charge of the kids, and off we flew.

We were greeted at Geneva Airport by Cal, Bu, and Thomas, their Jack Russell. The following Monday we were introduced to our interpreter, and we began a five-day marathon of classes by day and counseling in the evenings. Every meal was a time of listening and ministry. It was great! I am still humbled that God would trust us to minister to some of His dearest servants. We left a part of our hearts there at the YWAM Training Center.

The second week we stayed in Cal and Bu's home. It was so good to be with them. They took us all over Switzerland. We dined in quaint restaurants and visited ancient churches, villages, castles and walled cities. I wore my green John Deere jacket and my best ball cap to the top of the Alps. We had gone as far up as the train could take us. It was surely a high that God intended us to experience. From the observation deck we could see a lone climber going yet higher up the pure white mountain slope. We often see ourselves like that lone climber, only a speck in the vastness of God's creation. "But we are His workmanship, created in Christ Jesus unto good works, which God hath before ordained that we should walk in them" (Ephesians 2:10).

CHAPTER 35

Courthouse Steps

A unity rally on the courthouse steps during the 1980s was called in order to promote unity in our greatly divided community. The sponsoring organization had asked me as convenor of the Orangeburg Area Ministers' Fellowship to speak along with others including the mayor, police chief, and more. After a stirring message from the President of the Black Ministerial Alliance, I was introduced as the President of the White Ministers' Fellowship. After my short message, I descended the courthouse steps and an elderly black lady said to me, "There ought to be no such thing as separate black and white ministers' groups in our town!" I assured her that the introduction was inaccurate and that she was absolutely right. According to God's Word, we all are one in Christ. If the pastors can't get together, how in the world would the community ever be in unity. Wow!

I relayed this experience at our next Ministers' Fellowship meeting and the dialogue became very exciting. A group of us, including the local president of the NAACP, decided to attend the next meeting of the Black Ministerial Alliance with the notion that if God wanted our community to walk in unity, then we as ministers of the gospel should set the example. It quickly became evident the principalities and powers over our city did not want unity because for three months we tried to get on the Alliance's agenda, only to find the meeting canceled or moved to an undisclosed location at the last moment. Finally, we crashed their meeting at a local church and stated our case. We wanted to dissolve our fellowship and join their group without holding any office as a show of unity to them and our community. We further stated our belief that the Lord would bless our faith and determination to stand together for the healing of the racial division in our community.

The alliance listened, then excused themselves for an executive session. They soon returned and the president expressed the decision of the group to reject our offer because they wanted to keep their black identity, heritage and culture intact.

Years have passed. I am very disappointed to report that except for facades and tokenism, no real change has taken place. Sunday morning is still the most segregated time of the week in our city! "How can two walk together except they agree?" (Amos 3:3).

We all have heritage and we all follow culture to a certain degree, but what about the culture of Christ? John told those who asked about his mission "No one can receive anything unless God gives it from heaven. You yourselves know how plainly I told you, 'I am not the Messiah. I am only here to prepare the way for him.' It is the bridegroom who marries the bride, and the best man is simply glad to stand with him and hear his vows. Therefore, I am filled with joy at his success. He must become greater and greater, and I must become less and less" (John 3:27-30, NLT).

Yes, he must increase and I must decrease! To me, that includes every facet of my life. I walk with Him and increasingly become more identified with Him.

Acts 6 reports on a situation that arose in the early church between two groups concerning the neglect of their widows. Instead of separating themselves from the complaining group, the apostles declared a solution that kept the focus of leadership intact and at the same time met the need of that people group. "That there should be no schism in the body; but that the members should have the same care one for another" (1 Corinthians 12:25).

To the dear little lady at the courthouse steps I can only say, "I am sorry!" It breaks my heart that the leadership focus was not on Christ nor the Kingdom of God, but on the will of men with a self-serving religious agenda.

CHAPTER 36

One on One

Not too long after the disappointing outcome of the Unity Rally, God brought a local black pastor into my life. I started meeting with Cedric, a Panamanian by birth, on Wednesdays for prayer and fellowship. One Wednesday I was recounting with him a recent conversation I had with another local pastor who was well known and well established in the community. We had talked about crossing racial boundaries and he admitted that he was uncomfortable around people of other races. He struggled to relate to them and to those of different cultures.

As Cedric and I discussed this issue, he mentioned that his denomination had developed a program to bridge the gap between races and cultures. That was good news! At our next Ministers' Fellowship meeting, we asked if anyone would be interested in committing a block of time to this program. Several expressed their interest, including the pastor who had earlier shared with me about his discomfort.

We sent out a notice to our entire mailing list of around two hundred. As I remember, we ended up with eight or ten pastors who would make the commitment to be paired with a person of a different race, meet weekly to discuss the weekly assignment, and meet monthly as a group for a teaching and challenge. This would continue for nine months.

"One on One" was designed to build relationships across racial and cultural lines. It entailed many difficult and uncomfortable assignments, but was definitely life-changing. I am happy to report that everyone kept their commitment and everyone said that the experience was a great benefit. I am confident that every one of the participants has a newfound freedom in Christ. I wish that more of our community's pastors would have participated in this life changing journey, but I thank God for those who did. This was not just a program, but good seed sown into our lives that I pray will continue to bring forth much good fruit!

CHAPTER 37

Women in Ministry

Regretfully, one of the annual debates at our presbytery meetings was about women in ministry, especially those in leadership roles. During that time in my life as a young presbyter, Brother Ken Sumrall told me during a brief encounter to always keep a message ready in the back of my Bible because he might call on me one day to preach it. I was never called on to preach that message, but I did follow his example of preparing someone to always be ready to minister. I told a deaconess in our church the same thing. Many other leaders could prepare a message for future use, but this lady could get up at any time, ready and willing to minister from God's Word.

One Sunday morning something happened that had never happened before or since. The Sheriff's dispatcher sent me a 911 page, "needed at ER now!" As I stepped down from the pulpit, the deaconess stepped up. Out the parking lot I drove. I got to the ER just in time to sit down on the hallway floor with a young deputy and break the terrifying news that his young daughter had suddenly died! I was where I needed to be, the deaconess was where she needed to be and both ministries were functioning.

Where would we be or what would we miss if it were not for faithful women in the church? We have many faithful men in leadership, but that does not mean we can discount the women just because of gender. "For you are all children of God through faith in Christ Jesus. And all who have been united with Christ in baptism have put on the character of Christ, like putting on new clothes. There is no longer Jew or Gentile, slave or free, male and female. For you are all one in Christ Jesus. And now that you belong to Christ, you are the true children of Abraham. You are his heirs, and God's promise to Abraham belongs to you" (Galatians 3:26-29, NLT).

Are we willing to limit women's uninhibited praise and worship, their relentless prayer and intercession, or the compassion and nurturing that naturally flows from their heart? What about the revelation God has given women concerning His Word and His ways? I was blessed to have anointed faithful men in leadership, but many churches did not nor do not, so where would those churches be without the women that God has called and anointed for ministry? I probably wouldn't do well in a theological debate on this topic, but I know how Bethel Church has been blessed because we did not limit women in ministry as some others have. One excellent book on this subject is David Joel Hamilton and Loren Cunningham's *Why Not Women?*
A Fresh Look at Scripture on Women in Missions, Ministry, and Leadership.

SECTION FIVE

CHAPTER 38

Sunday Morning Rabbits

I stepped out the back door in my dark grey three-piece suit only to see the whole back yard covered with white rabbits. They were under the vehicles and in the bushes—everywhere except in their pen where they belonged!

I usually went to church earlier than the rest of the family, but on this particular Sunday I had to get everyone up to help round up these bunnies before we could do anything else. The kids loved it. When we had accomplished the task, I managed to recover my ministerial look and manner before entering church.

The only other time I had more rabbit fur on me was years later when, as chaplain, I was asked to ride the Easter bunny into the local mall on a four wheeler while wearing my black Sheriff's Office uniform. I guess someone had leaked the story about my previous encounter with the bunnies. Who else could manage a 200-pound bunny with arms of white artificial fur wrapped around you? The waiting crowd of kids really loved it: an Easter bunny being delivered by a sheriff's four wheeler with blue lights flashing. We managed to get this extra large bunny safely off the machine and standing on two feet. He straightened his ears and began tossing candy to the anxious crowd. In both cases my clothes looked like I had been wrestling with the abominable snowman!

Follow That Dream

I have learned that life goes a lot easier when you can laugh at yourself. I am reminded of a young father who came back from ministerial training so serious and pious. He really struggled with having fun. I guess he had all his fun before he came to Christ. We were having a baptismal service by the bridge at a local creek. Since it was a "church service," this minister wore his standard white starched shirt and three-piece black suit. It was sweltering hot, but the water temperature of the black water creek was somewhere between cold and colder. After baptizing a variety of folks, we all, except the brother in the black suit, had a grand time jumping, splashing and swimming in the chilly water. I looked up toward the bank just in time to see him, with a scowl on his face, telling his wife, "I wish I could have fun like that." To which his wife replied, "You could if you weren't such an old stick in the mud!" With that he ordered his kids out of the creek, loaded them in the car and took off.

A few minutes later, I saw an approaching cloud of dust and heard the scream of the engine. It was our dear pious brother! His car slid to a halt on the bridge above as we all stood in the chest-deep water below with our mouths wide open. He flung himself off the bridge, three piece suit and all!

Deliverance of self comes in many forms and fashion. Life and ministry are to be enjoyed, not endured. The Lord is not giving His ministers and their families a torture test. "A cheerful heart is good medicine, but a broken spirit saps a person's strength" (Proverbs 17:22, NLT). Lighten up!

CHAPTER 39

On the Coldest Winter Nights

It always turned out to be one of the coldest nights of winter when Tripp and I were going camping. Judy thought we planned it that way, but we did not. It just always seemed to happen. Any father who has promised his young son a camping trip then tries to convince him that its too cold to camp outside knows you just have to "man up" and go. Besides, we had sleeping bags, tents, and all the provisions we needed. The early pioneers did it without all that modern stuff.

It's sometimes tough being tough. Our first order of business was convincing each other that "it ain't so bad out here!" After our heads were in the right place, we had to put up the tent and build a fire. One night it was so cold, in the teens as I remember, that we should have built the fire two days before in the hopes of getting the place warm.

Farnum boys had been camping in this spot along the creek, where the old mill house once stood, for generations. Now it was up to us to carry on the family tradition.

Cooking over an open fire, telling stories and just being together with your son is wonderful. One of the stories I like to tell was about the time when, as a boy, I was camping with my buddies in the very same spot during the summer. We had decided to fry chicken using the "candy" recipe I learned at the hunting club. All was going well. As we anxiously waited for the first pan to be ready, a thunderstorm came out of nowhere. It rained so hard that the grease splashed into the open fire and the whole thing went up in sky-high flames. We jumped out of the tent, kicked over the frying pan and salvaged the half-cooked chicken from the ground. As the rain persisted, we retreated to my home where Mom cleaned all the pine straw and leaves off the chicken and finished frying it for us. She was a real trooper!

On another occasion we were having a father-son campout at the same location. I think there were eight of us present; others had dropped out because the weather had turned so cold. Imagine that! It was so cold that you could take boiling stew, put it on a plate and not have to wait for it to cool down before eating it! This time, we were sitting around the campfire waiting for the stew to be ready. One of the fathers was wearing loafers and complained that his feet were freezing cold. As he put his shoe soles close to the roaring fire, a smile of delight appeared on his face. In a few minutes I noticed that his shoe soles were smoking and suggested that he pull his feet back a little. Nothing doing, the heat felt too good! In just a few more seconds, everyone except him burst out laughing because the glue in his shoes melted and the soles came unglued from the toe, drooping down and looking like ears on a hound dog. Those were great times.

I haven't camped with my son in years, but we still get around the fire on occasion and tell the funny stories. I am blessed to still have good times with him and all my kids! "Children are a gift from the Lord; they are a reward from him. Children born to a young man are like arrows in a warrior's hands. How joyful is the man whose quiver is full of them" (Psalm 127:3-5, NLT).

CHAPTER 40

Willing to be Wrong

"They weren't always right, but they were never wrong!" This saying seemed to perfectly describe a specific family in our community. If you wanted to get a fight started, just make a matter of fact statement to them. No matter what the subject, the scrap was on. I was not quick to go to blows, but I had a definite opinion about things and a quick tongue to match.

Early in my Christian walk, the Lord asked me one day if I was willing to be wrong. "Wrong about what?" I wondered. "Oh, anything or everything I may ask of you," the Lord replied.

I soon came to understand that He was asking me if I would be willing to change my attitude. The Lord wasn't asking me to be a wimp, neither was He asking me to not have an opinion, clear core values or a precise belief system. He simply wanted me to understand that my attitude at the beginning of a situation or encounter would greatly influence or dictate the outcome. This is certainly true when it comes to relationships. Instead of preaching my clear and often sharp opinion early in a relationship, I can learn about the other person by listening to them. Their story is always more important than mine. This attitude and practice often earn me the right to tell my story later.

I have been privileged to be included in ecumenical services in our community many times. I had a brief encounter with another area minister just days before one of those events. He began to tell me what he was going to say and how he was going to say it and that they may never invite him back, but he was going to tell them the truth! You guessed it, they never invited him back! In the midst of his zeal to tell things the way he believed them to be, he forgot about grace.

The cry of St. Francis, "First to understand and then to be understood," surely applies to our attitudes and how we relate to others. What we see as a simple crossing of paths could be a divine encounter. As the Lord sent Philip to the Ethiopian eunuch, the Lord will send us to go near and join ourselves to someone's chariot. (Acts 8:27-39) You or I may not be caught up, but the journey will be very exciting and we can rejoice that the Lord chose us for the occasion. Now, I'll ask you what the Lord asked me, "Are you willing to be wrong?"

CHAPTER 41

Our God is Faithful

Judy and I were looking for a home for our growing family. We kept being drawn to this one house that was on one and a half acres of fenced property. Everything was out of our price range, even the house we were renting at the time for one hundred twenty-five dollars a month! In spite of that, we had a promise from the Lord. "Establish my house first and then I will establish yours."

We had been diligent to get the church established. We had purchased an old home on Ellis Avenue for the church and had plans on the drawing board for a new facility in a different location. We started a building fund campaign and sold church bonds. Everything was going our way except the interest rates. During this time in the 80s, interest on real estate loans spiked up to 15½ percent for a short while. I was not surprised that the banks called us crazy to believe God for provision, but I was surely disappointed when our church elders were divided over moving forward. That lack of consensus brought our building program to a grinding halt.

The advantage that these high interest rates brought was the fact that no one could sell anything, especially the home we had been riding by and praying over for six months. Have you ever experienced a time when you had no options except what God provided? That's the best place to

One Couple's Journey

be! There is a country song that describes my basic attitude about receiving, even from God. "I ain't asking nobody for nothing, I'll just get it on my on!"

That attitude may sound good and noble, but this time the Lord wanted to teach me more about receiving. Soon after we came back to town to establish Bethel, a brother came to the podium after the service and laid down a set of keys. "The Lord told me to give you this car!"

"I don't need a car, the one I have is just fine," I said almost automatically. Actually, the car he was trying to give me, an almost brand new Country Squire station wagon, was much finer than my car. Based on my response, Cal reluctantly retrieved the keys and went home.

The next Sunday he came up again, but this time in tears. "The Lord told me to give you this car and here are the keys!" I'm telling you that this guy didn't normally cry. We submitted and picked up the wagon, full of gas, fully detailed with signed title. Several days later our fine Oldsmobile started coming apart.

God had provided a car and He also seemed to be determined to provide a house for the Farnum family. As interest rates stayed up, the sale price of this house kept coming down. While chatting one day with a friend, I told him that we were praying about buying this house but there was no way we would be able to secure enough down payment to get the monthly payments down to an affordable amount. Several days later my friend called and said it was all worked out through a relative of his who attended Bethel when they were in town. In just a matter of days we were handed a check for a $30,000 personal loan to be paid back whenever we were able.

Today, I am writing from our study in that home. Our children, grandchildren and great grandson call this Gan Gan and Pa Pa's house. As a bonus, our home is located on a drive named for my German grandmother. I am not special nor am I bragging, but I am saying that God is faithful, and all His promises are yea and amen! (2 Corinthians 1:20).

CHAPTER 42

You're Not Listening to Me!

"You're not listing to me!"

"Yes, I am."

"Okay. Then what did I just say?"

It was late at night. I was tired and she was upset. Does it sound familiar? Judy and I had been married twenty years and she had been trying to get my attention for quite some time. It seems I had time for everyone and everything except her.

She was right, but I didn't know how to break the cycle. While I was always busy providing for our family and ministry, she had always been a very faithful and diligent wife, mother of five, homemaker and pastor's wife and anything else anyone needed. As mentioned in a previous chapter, I had given myself to other community and extra local ministries while at the same time being pastor of Bethel.

While driving home from a monthly preaching and teaching trip to several churches in North Carolina, several things were happening. I was mentally wrestling with both her feelings and mine. The closer I got to home, the more intense they became. The Lord interrupted this wrestling match with a clear admonishment, "If you invested as much in your relationship with Judy as you do in these churches, your stomach wouldn't feel like it had a brick in it!"

I was serving as a presbyter for a large charismatic fellowship, a district overseer for a number of churches in North Carolina, South Carolina and Georgia, and the convener of our local ministers' fellowship, as well as serving on various committees and community projects. Ministry, like any other profession, can become a jealous mistress that causes us to get our priorities out of line. The Lord made it clear to me that my wife and our relationship of 20-plus years was far more important than all those "ministries." That day, I repented before God and asked him to help me to change.

We were both struggling in our relationship. She needed to be able to express her needs and I needed to learn to listen. It's funny how we can listen to everyone except the one we love the most. We immediately reestablished our date night and talked and listened to each other for hours on end. The Lord helped us establish a safe place for the two of us as our understanding of each other and Him became deeper and richer. There were lots of tears and blessings as our relationship became more wonderful than ever!

I would want to say this to any couple that is struggling. Don't give up. Learn to do battle with the problem, not with each other! Judy was not my enemy, nor was I hers. I couldn't just blame this situation on the devil, but he is our common enemy who wanted to kill, steal and destroy all that we had together and the plans God had for our lives

(John 10:10). Judy and I still loved each other very much, but we had gotten out of touch with each other. There was no other person involved, only the jealous mistress of ministry to everyone else but my wife.

Years before the farm had been the jealous mistress in our relationship. I gradually fell into this trap. Before we knew it, we were taking one another for granted. If this attitude persists, the relationship usually spirals downward. Our turnaround started with my encounter with the Lord's still small voice. I repented and set a different course. Like David, I asked the Lord to create in me a clean heart and renew a right spirit in me (Psalms 51:10). A right spirit in this situation was to seek Judy out and spend quality time with her.

The goal of marriage is not to merely survive, but to thrive! For any marriage to thrive, both husband and wife must practice the God-kind of love by giving and receiving mutual support and trust. At the marriage altar we both testified that we believed in our hearts that we had found the one person that we could unconditionally love. That is the God-kind of love! (John 3:16).

Just as Christ is the centerpiece for God's unconditional love for the world, Christ must be the centerpiece of our life and marriage. He alone can successfully guide and direct our individual lives and marriage. Our love for each other must be expressed daily through simple and practical acts of love. One of those is listening to each other's dreams, fears, ideas, cares and concerns. Our greatest expression of love is that of sacrificial giving. That is, following God's example of His perfect love by taking that which is solely ours and sharing it with our mate. In the marriage covenant, that means our two lives became one. Next to our commitment to Christ, our marriage covenant is life's greatest investment and will pay life's greatest returns and fulfillment.

Being faithful to God and faithful to each other keeps our love fresh, rich and growing. God's Word tells us that this faithful kind of love is patient; it is kind and envies no one. Love is never boastful, nor conceited, nor rude, never selfish, not quick to take offense. Love keeps no score of wrongs; does not gloat over men's sins, but delights in the truth. There is nothing love cannot face; there is no limit to its faith, its hope and its endurance. (1 Corinthians 13).

That same year on April 8, 2015 we celebrated our 48th wedding anniversary!

CHAPTER 43

Out on Visitation

I was "out on visitation," fishing in a backwater area, when I hooked a small bass. As I was attempting to get the small treble hook out of the frisky little rascal's mouth, he fluttered and then we were both hooked. The fish's movement worked the barb deeper into my thumb before I could release him and begin to unhook myself. I cut the small wire treble hook off the lure before I proceeded in attempting to pull the hook out of my thumb. I first stuck my hand down into my cooler until it was thoroughly numb before I tried to remove the hook from my hand. But I could not get it out because I had cut the shank too short. Since my thumb was still numb, I thought, "I can live with this!"

That idea soon proved to be crazy, so I headed for the landing. After loading the boat, I was driving out of the parking lot, again thinking maybe the hook would dissolve or something, when my "hooked" thumb got jammed by the steering wheel. I could vaguely see my phone through the water in my eyes as I called our church secretary and told her that things had not gone well while out on visitation. I asked her to please call her friend at the doctor's office and see if he could work me in his schedule.

By the time I got to the doctor's office my thumb was throbbing up to my elbow. It was mid-afternoon and I was the only one in the waiting room. (That should have been a clue). After a short wait I was escorted to a room in the back and soon after the doctor came in. Looking at my thumb, he said that he "hadn't seen one of these for a while." He proceeded to rummage through an old cabinet, emerging with something that looked like a tooth extractor. The doctor made his try at the hook and I almost kicked him out of his chair. "Hey, Doc, I could have done that myself. We need to rethink this approach" I shouted.

After determining that what he was trying to do would not work, he instructed his nurse to prepare a shot of Novocain to deaden the thumb and to check in an old toolbox to see if she could find a pair of pliers. The doctor stuck the needle in my thumb and pushed the plunger. Half the dose squirted back in my face. "Well, that ought to be enough," he said. "We'll just wait a minute or so for it to go into effect."

His first tug at the hook was in the wrong direction. My thought of just letting the hook stay in there and rot out seemed very reasonable at that time. We came to a mutual agreement, and he put in a second shot of Novocain. This time my thumb felt twice its size. I think he could have cut the entire thumb off without me feeling it. Doc did surgery with those old needle-nose pliers, and I was out of there! The Lord spoke to me about my foolishness in thinking that I could live the rest of my life with a fishhook in my thumb.

One Couple's Journey

Life often has sharp barbs that become embedded in us. After the initial shock or numbness wears off, that pain becomes a constant distraction. As we focus on our pain, or trying to protect ourselves from being hurt again, life becomes no fun. In time, blame and anger will be our strategy for dealing with our pain, whether it be physical or emotional.

There are two basic sources of pain in our lives: what others do to us and what we do to ourselves. The Lord Jesus is the answer to whatever the pain, no matter where it comes from. Jesus is the great physician. He is not having to "practice" medicine.

"Then the Pharisees went out, and held a council against him, how they might destroy him. But when Jesus knew it, he withdrew himself from thence: and great multitudes followed him, and he healed them all" (Matthew 12:14-15).

Go to Him quickly with your hurts. Receive His healing and deliverance.

The other lesson? Remember what some pastors could actually be doing when the secretary says they are "out on visitation."

CHAPTER 44

Deep Down Hurt and Anger

Deep down under the surface was a pool of anger in me that had not erupted in a long time. I sat at the conference table listening to two seasoned men of God who had walked together for years, leading the charge in opposite directions over age-old issues. It felt like what Pete said in the movie Lonesome Dove, "Can we eat now, or do we have to wait 'til the argument is over?"

In years prior, the questions and debate would emerge during our presbytery meeting and the passions would flare. One would hold to the traditions of the past and the other spoke of the future and the uncharted waters of change. One came from a theological ideal, the other from a pioneering spirit.

Something began to stir in me as I watched and listened to these two elder churchmen present their cases. Their postures touched a time in my childhood when I stood between my mom and dad as they argued about where Mom had hidden Dad's liquor bottle. Those many years ago, I had pleaded with them to stop arguing with tears in my eyes. But it was to no avail. Daddy was never mean, nor physically abusive, but was only trying to deal with his own pain. All I knew to do was to run and try to find a safe place. As a boy, I sat on the top rail of the lot fence where the farm animals heard my cry and vowed that as long as I lived, I would never drink and expose the ones I loved to such hurt and fear.

As it was when I was a boy, I made my appeal with tears to these two seasoned leaders, but to no avail. "We have found the enemy and the enemy is us," an insightful person once wrote. I traveled home under a cloud of concern. The divide widened and the split ensued. Brothers in Christ who had stood together in battle to advance the Kingdom now were forced to choose sides or just walk away. It was devastating for me. I later wished that I had never chosen a side and could have somehow disconnected myself from that vision.

The Lord had led Judy and I to set a standard that still stands today, and I had expected no less from those I was submitted to. My anger was consuming me. A dear brother and confidant of mine accompanied me to a private meeting with the leader of one of those factions. The more we talked, the more angry I became. I literally walked away from the one I had looked to as a spiritual father.

Only Judy and a very few friends knew the depth of my despair. Of course, the Lord knew. He will never leave us as orphans nor without hope. He would send me an unlikely ally who would give me a diversion until my vision became clear again and the anger within was extinguished. "And be renewed in the spirit of your mind; And that ye put on the new man, which after God is created in righteousness and true holiness. Wherefore putting away lying, speak every man truth with his neighbor: for we are members one of another. Be ye angry, and sin not: let not the sun go down upon your wrath: Neither give place to the devil" (Ephesians 4:23-27).

CHAPTER 45

Fishing with Frank

I ran into Mr. Frank at the fishing tackle isle. As a boy I remembered seeing him at the country store where Mom and Dad would stop for a beer in the evenings. A Marine survivor of the battle of Guadalcanal, Mr. Frank was a retired farm equipment salesman.

Our brief conversation turned from the old days with Frog and Gertie (Dad & Mom) to bass fishing. "Do you ever do any fishing?" Frank asked.

"Na, I'm too busy with family and the church," I replied.

"Well, if you ever want to go, let me know."

When our paths crossed again, a second invitation was given. I was around forty years old and had recently lost another father figure in my life. I was semi-depressed from years of not seeing the success that I expected. In farming terms, I had several short crops. It takes just as much energy to make a short crop as it does a bunker crop.

The difference is the expected or needed return is not enough. Like Moses, I had too many people at my tent door, and I thought I was supposed to be the answer for all their needs. (Exodus 18:17-18)

So, with Judy's encouragement, I began a weekly fishing trip with Frank. This went on for the next several years. Frank gave me all sorts of tackle and fishing gear, but most of all, he gave me a much needed diversion, a hobby, a "safe place" of unconditional acceptance in which he never asked for anything in return. Frank did agree one time that when either one of us caught a fish, I would say "hallelujah" and if we missed a fish, he would say "damn." Frank was not a preacher, nor a counselor. He was a friend sent by God to me and my family.

Sometimes Frank would show up at our house early Saturday mornings. He would bring doughnuts, wake up all the kids, have a fast cup of coffee, make us all laugh and then be gone. Just a quickly as he disappeared on those Saturday mornings, Mr. Frank died suddenly.

Judy, the kids, and I are so thankful for Mr. Frank and a very few others like him who came into our lives in times of need and gave us real encouragement. If we are not careful, we can miss a blessing by dismissing a person God sends. "Be not forgetful to entertain strangers: for thereby some have entertained angels unawares" (Hebrews 13:2).

For me, there would be no more fathers. Now I was being challenged by God to be a father figure to others instead. I thank the Lord for all the wonderful examples He gave me and for all the experiences I had with fathers, both good and bad.

CHAPTER 46

Angel Called

One busy Sunday morning our young grandson Wes answered the phone. At the conclusion of the brief phone conversation, he found his Grandmother Judy and said, "Grandpa really does know angels!"

"He sure does," Judy answered. "What makes you say that right now?"

Wes went on to explain that an angel had just asked for Grandpa on the phone and gave him the message that she would not be in church that morning!

To many, church is a mystical thing that seems far from everyday living. My life would be without form and void without the two institutions our God established: marriage and church. Without marriage I wouldn't have many precious memories like the one of my young grandson thinking he was talking to a real angel—who by the way was a real person named Angel. Likewise, without the church, I wouldn't be connected to Christ's body as God intended.

One of the governing principles of my life is that we all need to be part of something that is bigger than we are so that we don't just belong to the kingdom of self. I keep a small box on my dresser with visual reminders that my life is not my own. It is His, bought with a price. Those visual reminders in the box include a small cross, military service medals, a state and national flag, pinnate and collar brass from the World Trade Center, just to name a few. "What? know ye not that your body is the temple of the Holy Ghost which is in you, which ye have of God, and ye are not your own? For ye are bought with a price: therefore glorify God in your body, and in your spirit, which are God's" (1 Corinthians 6:19-20).

Church is where we get equipped for the life of service God has called us to. Church is a place where we can learn to appreciate God's grace and mercy as we relate to His body of which we are all members. "And he gave some, apostles; and some, prophets; and some, evangelists; and some, pastors and teachers; For the perfecting of the saints, for the work of the ministry, for the edifying of the body of Christ: Till we all come in the unity of the faith, and of the knowledge of the Son of God, unto a perfect man, unto the measure of the stature of the fulness of Christ" (Ephesians 4:11-13).

As a pastor growing a young energetic church, the Lord allowed me to understand that the church was also growing a pastor. Judy and I and our children have all seen and felt the good, the bad and the ugly of church life. With that being said, I know that God inhabits the praises of His people. We all yearn for the day when His body will be without spot or blemish. Until that time comes, we have at least one angel in our midst!

CHAPTER 47

Family Time

At the end of your life, who will miss you? Family time is the most important time in your life next to time with God. Period. There is a thin line between providing for your family and just being away.

It was early Thanksgiving Day morning, 2013. Judy and I were up later than usual the night before. We were in the kitchen doing our usual Thanksgiving routine. Most of our kids and grandkids would be home the next day. It's okay if the fixings are not just right, the important thing is that we are together as a family.

I think back to the Thanksgivings when I ate Thanksgiving dinner on the tailgate, in the field. For whatever reason we were running behind on harvesting crops and had to get the work done. Judy understood to some degree and our young kids thought it was a great adventure.

Different families have different Thanksgiving traditions. As a boy I remember quail hunting with my dad. Later after my two sisters were married, their husbands joined in for quail hunt or a short deer drive after dinner. When the hunt was over, we would return to the house for a second round of leftovers. For Judy and I and the kids, it has become harder and harder to get everybody together on major holidays much less in between. Some live far away, all have their own families, the in-laws need their time, and on and on. There are many valid reasons.

It could be our own fault. We raised our kids to be independent and we are thankful that they are sustaining themselves. Judy and I were accused of leaving our parents, siblings and wedding party in the church yard and never looking back or waving good-bye. So now we understand how they felt because our babies have grown up and spread their wings. Our hearts still yearn to see our "babies" and their babies, but we remind ourselves of God's blessing on our children's lives and His word that they should leave and cleave. They are living their dreams and enjoying their adventures as it should be.

Love your children. Support them as they follow the call towards their destiny. If they get off track like we did, be there for them and pray for them without ceasing. Life is shorter than we think, so love them while you can.

One of my greatest gifts at any time of the year is to have my kids near me, watch them interact, and see their children do the same. I hope you see children as one of God's greatest gifts. "Except the Lord build the house, they labor in vain that build it: except the Lord keep the city, the watchman waketh but in vain. It is vain for you to rise up early, to sit up late, to eat the bread of sorrows: for so he giveth his beloved sleep. Lo, children are an heritage of the Lord: and the fruit of the womb is his reward. As arrows are in the hand of a mighty man; so are children of the youth. Happy is the man that hath his quiver full of them: they shall not be ashamed, but they shall speak with the enemies in the gate" (Psalm 127:1-5).

SECTION SIX
CHAPTER 48

New Purpose

God will not leave us without hope. He opened a door of new purpose for me through a community tragedy. A city police officer was senselessly gunned down during a routine call. The family and entire community were devastated. A group of police chaplains came from another part of our state to help the department and the family during their time of bereavement. Their presence made a great impact on everyone involved.

When a community action group called People Against Crime was formed, the question emerged as to why we could not have our own police chaplains. Guess who was the only member of the clergy present. Yes, it was me. I was commissioned to find the answer. Little did I know at the time that the next two years would involve many hours of specialized training and the beginning of another twenty years of ministry that is still going on today.

Three other area ministers joined me in this new challenge. We had the ride of our lives.

The main thing we had in common was that we were pastors and we were community-minded. We worked together to do research and attend training wherever we could. We presented our Law Enforcement Chaplain's Program to the city Police Department and the county Sheriff's

Office. The Sheriff accepted our program immediately and the Police Department accepted it the following year. Once the program was announced, we were able to recruit several other pastors and begin their training. Our requirements were tough, but we only wanted those who would have a real heart for the ministry and were willing to cover their own expenses.

It was difficult to find training that went beyond a basic level, but the Lord brought the right people across our paths many times. "Ask, and it shall be given you; seek, and ye shall find; knock, and it shall be opened unto you: For everyone that asketh receiveth; and he that seeketh findeth; and to him that knocketh it shall be opened. Or what man is there of you, whom if his son ask bread, will he give him a stone? Or if he asks a fish, will he give him a serpent? If ye then, being evil, know how to give good gifts unto your children, how much more shall your Father which is in heaven give good things to them that ask him?" (Matthew 7:7-11).

CHAPTER 49

McMeeting

Another chaplain from our group and I were in Atlanta for a day-long seminar on death notifications. At lunch break we hooked up with a local chaplain who knew of a McDonald's within walking distance. As we got introduced over a burger, I began to share my desire for more advanced training in trauma response and critical incident debriefing. As it turned out, the gentleman across the table was the head of the Behavioral Science Department at the Georgia Police Academy. What a God moment!

I begin to quiz Gene about the cost and dates of his next available session. Forty-hour courses in both Peer Counseling and Critical Incident Debriefing were soon to be offered. The courses were free, but you had to provide your own food and lodging. The only problem was you had to be a resident of Georgia to attend the academy. Gene, seeing my disappointment, said he would see what he could arrange and give me a call.

When the opportunity opened, I was the only chaplain and the only non-resident among a large group of GBI agents. I loved every minute of those classes. At the end of the second course on Critical Incident Debriefing, Gene expressed his confidence in us and our ability to help those involved in critical incidents. God's timing is right. He will put people in our lives at strategic moments!

Several months later, on New Year's Eve, I was lying on the couch watching TV and listening to my county radio when I became alerted by some radio traffic that didn't sound good. Judy asked why I was getting dressed and I told her something was wrong. I had hardly gotten the words out of my mouth when dispatch called and said frantically that a state trooper had been shot on I-95 and one of our deputies was his ride-a-long for a special DUI enforcement.

As I nervously raced toward the scene, praying for God's wisdom and strength, I remembered Gene's words of confidence. They gave me courage. It is never good when cops cry. There is a lot that could be said about that first major incident for me, but that night another good man died in the line of duty. The lives of his partners and their families would never be the same. One young trooper in the crowd grabbed me, sobbing. It was all I could do to hold him up. Crying with him, I tried to reassure him that God would comfort and strengthen him, and he would make it through the loss of his close friend and mentor.

Several years later I accompanied our SWAT team for a day of training with other agencies at Fort Jackson Army Training Center. I was the only chaplain and the oldest person there. I was happy to join the grueling ropes course and I was determined not to quit or fall off as others had already done. It was a midlife crisis, "man it up" thing! Honestly, I was desperately hanging on to this rope while sliding down between two towers. This was probably the third back to back exercise after climbing and repelling off the high tower twice. All my breath and strength were gone with only a few more feet to go when I heard a loud voice from the crowd say, "Come on chaplain, you can make it!" Make it I did.

You guessed it. That same young trooper who I had encouraged years before was giving encouragement back to me. "Be not deceived; God is not mocked: for whatsoever a man soweth, that shall he also reap. For he that soweth to his flesh shall of the flesh reap corruption; but he that soweth to the Spirit shall of the Spirit reap life everlasting. And let us not be weary in well doing: for in due season we shall reap, if we faint not. As we have therefore opportunity, let us do good unto all men, especially unto them who are of the household of faith" (Galatians 6:7-10).

My eternal thanks to Gene for investing and believing in me and to the Lord who gave me so many opportunities to see Him work in the lives of others.

CHAPTER 50

'Phesians?

The deputy asked the mother for the name of her son who assaulted her. "Phesians," she replied. Not understanding, he asked again. "Phesians" she repeated.

"Ma'am, could you spell that for me?"

She spelled it out letter for letter: "E-p-h-e-s-i-a-n-s, just like in the Bible."

The deputy thanked her, finished gathering the information needed for his report, and we exited the home.

Back in his patrol car the deputy asked me if that name was really in the Bible. "Oh yeah," I answered. "It's the name of a New Testament book written by the Apostle Paul."

Back in those days I spent 40-plus hours every month in a patrol car. We were still trying to establish our credibility and not everyone was as comfortable with a chaplain as Clark was. When one other deputy was instructed to go by the squad room and pick up the chaplain for a ride-a-long, he fired back, "I don't want some damn preacher riding in my car!" I didn't take his attitude personally. With time, we became real buddies.

On this particular night with Clark, a simple question was asked and I answered it without a sermon about church attendance or going to hell. Now eighteen years later, I look back and remember how proud he was when he was promoted to Sergeant. He taught me street survival and I just served him as unto the Lord. We took many a fast ride together and had some tense moments from time to time. We sweated together, froze together, got soaked together, and once or twice we even enjoyed nice weather together! Most of all, we covered each other's backs. He wasn't perfect and neither am I, but the Bible says that love covers a multitude of sins. He was an ambitious young warrior, eager to learn and strove to be the best. Clark worked hard and set a tough but fair pace as he moved up the ranks.

The Bible says in Proverbs 27:17, "As iron sharpens iron, so a man sharpens the countenance of his friend." We shared articles and books with each other. We had great dialogues about the Lord, policing issues, leadership principles, marriage, and parenting, just to name a few. Several years after being promoted to Major, Clark moved on to another agency in another part of the state. We talk often and I am reminded that he once told Judy and I that his number one goal in life was to become a man of prayer! God is so good!

CHAPTER 51

Crack House Prayer

As usual, the cars slid into the yard from every possible angle, their doors flew open and deputies ran into the night towards their target. The element of surprise is absolutely necessary for any operation of this type to be successful. In a matter of seconds, the house and its occupants were secure and I made my way towards the house. I was requested, "Chap, would you watch these folks while I go help search the premises?"

"You a preacher?" one of the females lining the outside of the house asked. Everyone had been told to face the outside wall with their hands raised against it and not move. This one young lady among the dozen or so being detained turned her head in my direction and asked if I would pray for her and her addiction.

"Lieutenant, I'm going to take this one around the corner and pray with her."

"10-4"

Out of sight from the others, she told me about her crack addition and her desire to be set free. We prayed and I escorted her back to her spot on the wall.

Countless times I have had the privilege to pray for folks who are in trouble or who have lost a loved one either naturally or violently. You never know when or who it will be. Once, one of my teenage daughters visited me at the Sheriff's Office. We were in the warrant's office where several people, in handcuffs, were being processed before going back to the jail. I noticed Amy's uneasiness about her surroundings, so we stepped out into the hallway. Amy asked, "Dad, how can you stand being in this place with these people?"

"Honey, this is what I do," I answered. "If I'm not here, I'll miss the little windows of opportunity that God opens for me."

I remember well the first night I was invited to ride along with the narcotics task force. I got a warm welcome since I knew most everyone there. As the commander finished his usual briefing and riding assignments, he asked that the Chaplain offer a word of prayer for the group. The team members gave each other puzzled looks as if to ask, "What is it that the commander has not told us about this operation? Why do we need prayer before we start?"

That was the beginning of many operations with multiple agencies where I had the privilege of blessing these officers, their families and praying for everyone's safety. For those who didn't quite understand or accept the chaplain's role in their world, they never turned down the cold water or hot coffee and snacks we brought with us. Even cops are people. Jesus Himself would have offered them a cup of cool water. Being His disciple isn't all that complicated! "And whoever gives one of these little ones even a cup of cold water because he is a disciple, I tell you, he shall not lose his reward" (Matthew 10:42, MOFF).

CHAPTER 52

NBC Nightly News

It was a big surprise when NBC News called and said they wanted to do a segment on our Chaplain's Program at the Sheriff's Office. We were a diverse group of ministers, but the four of us had one goal in mind—to develop the best chaplaincy program possible. All the research, training and dedication had paid off. These men earned the title of Chaplain. They had spent an average of forty-plus hours a month at the Sheriff's Office. Much of that time was spent on ride-a-longs with the deputies. Each Chaplain had completed the Reserve Deputy Training Course yet chose not to be a commissioned officer. We reasoned that we wanted to be an asset to the deputies while on patrol, not a liability.

We required each Chaplain to be "familiar" with all the equipment in the patrol vehicles and all the weapons issued to the deputies and to wear body armor while on duty. Each of the four chaplains averaged between three hundred to four hundred hours of training. Deputies were very thankful that we were available for death notifications, death scenes or any call that had a high level of emotional display or trauma. I refer to these men as "Line Chaplains." We did the ceremonial part of chaplaincy also, but our main purpose was to be on the front line with the men and women of our agency. We purposed to be a "safe place" for them by being good listeners and maintaining absolute confidentiality with them. I guess that's why NBC was interested in the program.

NBC sent a crew to Orangeburg for two days of filming and interviewing. It was a bit strange having cameras mounted on the patrol car hood and on the driver's side dashboard, with lights shining in our faces as we rode the familiar streets and roads of our community followed by the NBC crew van. Mostly, Sergeant Whetstone and I shadowed other units as they responded to actual calls for service. Things were unusually slow and the film crew was complaining about not having any real action to cover, so we started using the forbidden "quiet" word to describe the situation.

Sure enough, in a matter of minutes, a call came out about a bomb threat at a local industry. As we rolled up to the rather large manufacturing facility, all the employees had been evacuated. Fire trucks and EMS were on scene ready for some action. Forgetting we were wired for sound, the Sergeant and I laughed as the film crew declined our offer to help us sweep the building for any suspicious boxes or packages. "Man, you could get killed doing that," one of them said.

It turned to be a routine employee-driven, let's-get-out-of-work bomb threat, but it gave us the action that the NBC crew was looking for. That segment on the news was truly a God thing. He wanted to put the spotlight on His servants. We had the opportunity to share briefly of the need to support those who keep us safe.

There are many unsung heroes in the law enforcement profession who quietly and faithfully do their duty. They don't want any big fanfare, but they could always use a pat on the back and a sincere "Thank you." Some officers die from a single bullet while many more die a little each day because of the emotional stressors inherent to their work.

Why not start today by praying for those who serve and protect your community. Find ways to say, "thank you" and encourage your circle of influence to do the same. "I exhort therefore, that, first of all, supplications, prayers, intercessions, and giving of thanks, be made for all men; For kings, and for all that are in authority; that we may lead a quiet and peaceable life in all godliness and honesty. For this is good and acceptable in the sight of God our Savior, Who will have all men to be saved, and to come unto the knowledge of the truth" (1 Timothy 2:1-4).

CHAPTER 53

Your Services are No Longer Needed

I wasn't surprised when the sheriff called me in and told me, "Your services are no longer needed!" I shook his hand from across the desk and thanked him for the opportunity to serve.

As far back as my family could remember, I am the only Farnum to get fired from a volunteer position. Even though our chaplain's program had been featured on the NBC nightly news, neither the sheriff nor I expected my firing to make the local news headlines the next morning. Someone equated it to the sheriff firing God! The following day two captains were fired for the same reason: telling the sheriff the truth.

Pastor Jamie Buckingham wrote a great book, The Truth Will Set You Free, but first it will make you real miserable! You can't be that close to a person or organization without seeing the hidden agendas and the injustices inflicted upon certain employees. I told all four sheriffs I served through the years the truth, even to my own harm. I had some brief exchanges with the sheriff who fired me about ethics, leadership principles, honesty and corruption. He mostly had a pompous answer to anything I questioned. Sometimes he would agree with me to my face, then roast me after I left.

Several years before my firing, I was summoned to the sheriff's office where I found six or eight local pastors already seated in a semicircle. The sheriff started telling us that his mandate for being elected was two-fold. One was to rid the county of crime and the other was to fight racism. The previous sheriff had accepted and installed four chaplains in the department, three white and one black. There was a strong implication from the current sheriff that our chaplain's Corp, and especially me, were racist. Amid all the "Amens" in the room I stood up and asked, "Who in this room besides me pastors an interracial church?" For the first time during the entire meeting, the room became quiet.

Knowing his objective, I asked the sheriff, "Sheriff, what would you like for me to do concerning getting these pastors involved in the chaplain's Corp?"

"Oh, ah, ah, whatever you required for the current chaplains will be fine," he answered.

I escorted the group to my office, gave them each a list of training and equipment requirements (we furnished our own in those days) and the official application. I never heard from any of them again.

Not long after my dismissal, that sheriff was indicted and sent to federal prison. It was sad. The first black sheriff in our county since reconstruction ended his career of public service in disgrace. It was a terrible setback for his people and all citizens of our county.

I have never been an activist but have just simply tried to lead by example. Of the four sheriffs I have served under, two have been a great disappointment to me and our county. They both failed the code and tainted the badge of honor that so many others have worn without fault.

The job of leading is not easy. It requires moral character, integrity, and just plain guts to do the right thing as well as doing things right. The two sheriffs that failed their office had at least two things in common. Firstly, they surrounded themselves with the wrong kind of people, like the false prophets who surrounded certain kings of old, telling them what they wanted to hear instead of what they needed to hear. Secondly, they used fear and intimidation to keep their employees in line with their self-serving agenda.

I pray that as God's leaders, we become neither of those! "But Jesus called them unto him, and said, "Ye know that the princes of the Gentiles exercise dominion over them, and they that are great exercise authority upon them. But it shall not be so among you: but whosoever will be great among you, let him be your minister; And whosoever will be chief among you, let him be your servant: Even as the Son of man came not to be ministered unto, but to minister, and to give his life a ransom for many" (Matthew 20:25-28).

CHAPTER 54

Closed Chapters

We all have or will experience closed chapters in our lives. It is easy to say, "When the Lord closes one door, He always opens another!" But I have not always found it easy to make the change.

It has been said that the greatest change agent in our lives is pain. Who wants to knowingly volunteer for some pain?

Now in my late 60s, I can assure you that life has many welcome and many unwelcome changes. I can't help but think about God leading His chosen people to the promised land and the miracles they witnessed. It's unbelievable that they wanted to go back to the way it used to be in Egypt because of the struggles they encountered! "And when Pharaoh drew nigh, the children of Israel lifted up their eyes, and, behold, the Egyptians marched after them; and they were sore afraid: and the children of Israel cried out unto the Lord. And they said unto Moses, Because there were no graves in Egypt, hast thou taken us away to die in the wilderness? wherefore hast thou dealt thus with us, to carry us forth out of Egypt? Is not this the word that we did tell thee in Egypt, saying, Let us alone, that we may serve the Egyptians? For it had been better for us to serve the Egyptians, than that we should die in the wilderness. And Moses said unto the people, Fear ye not, stand still, and see the salvation of the Lord, which he will shew to you today: for the Egyptians whom ye have seen today, ye shall see them again no more forever. The Lord shall fight for you, and ye shall hold your peace" (Exodus 14:10-14).

Yet, like the children of Israel, we often attempt to worm our way back into a door the Lord has closed.

Shortly after my discharge from the sheriff's office, I was encouraged by an old friend to join him in disaster response. Paul is a veteran hospital chaplain and a veteran disaster responder and trainer for the National Organization for Victim Assistance (NOVA). While continuing my church responsibilities I threw myself into disaster relief training. Once again, the Lord showed me favor and I was able to get a lot of training under my belt in a short period of time. I was furthermore recommended by Paul to become a member of NOVA's National Disaster Response Team. My previous experience and training gave me an edge, so I moved through the training quickly. I knew what it meant to be ready for anything at any time.

When I was having breakfast with my long-time friend with SLED (state police), both our pagers went off almost simultaneously. The World Trade Center had been attacked and we both were on standby for different reasons.

I came home and begin checking my duty bag while watching the live coverage. My friend Paul responded to the World Trade Center emergency immediately to help assess the response needs for NOVA and five days later I relieved him. I had recently come back to the Sheriff's Office under a newly elected Sheriff. The Sheriff put me in an unmarked car, gave me one hundred dollars from his pocket and told me to "get to New York." My assignment there was the Central Precinct of Port Authority Police, who had lost thirteen officers.

During my time at Ground Zero there was still an around-the-clock effort to dig out survivors. They would not give up on their friends! Many stories could be told but I will simply say "they were the best, during the worst!" On my third night there, I had returned to my bunk in midtown after another long emotion-filled day. I began taking off my uniform. As I looked down, I noticed all the ash that was stuck to my boots and my pant legs from the knee down. I was standing there wondering how I would ever get them washed off. But the bigger question was how I would ever get all that I had seen, heard, tasted and smelled washed out of me. I had been sitting on the edge of Ground Zero by the I-beam cross, trying to wrap my head around the fact that I was right next to the grave of an estimated six thousand people.

Across the sight among the giant desolated buildings stood a tiny little church with hardly a shingle missing. Awesome! I learned one important thing during this process: you can't help people from a distance. You have to touch them. When you touch them, some of them gets on you! You can't wash it off; it becomes a part of you. "For even the Son of man came not to be ministered unto, but to minister, and to give his life a ransom for many" (Mark 10:45). This became evident when I returned home.

CHAPTER 55

Full Moon Birthday

Our Father never ceases to amaze me. Here I was in New York City just days after the 9/11 attack on the World Trade Center, looking at a beautiful full moon from the top of the Empire State Building. The building was shut down for security reasons, but my trauma response partner from the Baptist Mission where we were staying and I were given a private tour. Out of all the people in NYC that night, we were the only ones on top of the Empire State Building! And there it was, the biggest full moon I had ever seen!

I immediately thought, "I wish Judy were here to see this moon." It was her birthday, so I called her. "Happy Birthday honey, I bet you don't know where I am!"

"I never know where you are," she replied.

"I'm on top of the Empire State Building looking at this great big full moon and thinking of you," I said. Judy was on our patio in Orangeburg looking at the same moon! That was a special gift for Judy's birthday. Love is like that. It's the unplanned calls or notes that mean the most. I thank God for that moment of renewal during such a physical and emotion draining time of my life. I also gained some needed points with Judy!

CHAPTER 56

"Dad, Look Around!"

We had the largest table in a popular downtown Charleston restaurant with all our adult kids when one of them asked, "Dad, how was it at World Trade?" Amidst the hustle and bustle of that breakfast crowd I quietly began to tell the short version of my experiences. As much as I tried to fight back the tears, they began to flow. After a few minutes, one of my daughters interrupted me and said, "Dad, look around." At that moment, I realized that all eyes were on me. You could hear a pin drop in that restaurant. All of us were in pain because our nation had been attacked.

Judy and the kids have always been my best support group and they knew I needed to tell my story. We were in Charleston for the wedding of a classmate and dear friend of our girls. When I returned from New York, I had just enough time to change my travel bag contents and grab my robe and Bible before driving to Charleston to meet the kids. The groom's family were all from Nevada, so only the bride's family knew us very well. Just minutes before this old plantation courtyard wedding, I met with the groom and his father. Charlie asked me if I would pray for our nation during the time when I was praying to bless their marriage.

One Couple's Journey

As they knelt before me at the altar, I took a moment to express the couple's wishes, but I did not give any indication of my recent response to World Trade. As I began to pray, I began to weep. In another place and setting, the interviewer asked a psychologist friend and I how we were affected by responding to so much human tragedy. "We weep a lot," he replied.

I was privileged to once again return to New York the following February to serve the NYC Police and Fire departments. I thank the Lord for the opportunities to serve Him. I only remember one night in my entire career I complained as I was crawling out my bed for the third time to respond to dispatches requests for the chaplain. I groaned, "Oh Lord not again!" As clear as day the Lord responded, "Yes, again!" In His wonderful Fatherly way, He reminded me that I had prayed for the opportunity to be His servant in this place. I repented as I drove off into the night to my next assignment. You only have passion for what you do when you love what you do!

CHAPTER 57

Staying with Mickey

You may remember the year that the state of Florida had four hurricanes back to back. I was called on to do crisis intervention after two of those storms. The second response landed me and my team in Osceola County. It was late evening when I arrived to check in with the disaster response coordinator where we got our work assignments and housing information.

Well now, you're staying with Mickey!" she said.

"Mickey who?" I asked.

"That would be Mickey Mouse," was her reply.

"Are you kidding me?"

"Nope! It just so happens that all the storms have created a lot of cancellations at Disney World and they have available rooms, power and water. So that is where you will stay."

In my years of disaster response, I've rolled out my sleeping bag on every kind of floor imaginable, mostly concrete. This time it was going to be clean sheets at Mickey's!

Our assignment was to assist local government workers who were taking care of the elderly. This dedicated staff had continued to serve their clientele day after day for months without taking care of themselves. Many of those staff members had heavily damaged homes or no homes left at all. When I train crisis response volunteers, I always emphasize that our personal comfort is not an issue. We are there to serve people in crisis and not expect food or shelter above the situations we enter. Every once in a while, you may get to stay with Mickey, but normally you'll be eating disaster food and sleeping on a floor in a church building or some other local storm shelter.

The Apostle Paul had many credits to his name, but he constantly referred to himself as the servant of the Lord. Paul had learned how to be the Lord's servant. "How I praise the Lord that you are concerned about me again. I know you have always been concerned for me, but you didn't have the chance to help me. Not that I was ever in need, for I have learned how to be content with whatever I have. I know how to live on almost nothing or with everything. I have learned the secret of living in every situation, whether it is with a full stomach or empty, with plenty or little. For I can do everything through Christ, who gives me strength. Even so, you have done well to share with me in my present difficulty" (Philippians 4:10-14).

Needing to "rough it" is no big deal when you think about how rough the Lord Jesus had it. He was determined to do His Father's will and give His life a ransom for others. We find this in Mark 10:45. The same should be true for you and me. I never left a disaster site that my life was not richer and fuller than when I arrived. In that role I have witnessed so many miracles, the transformation of many lives, and so much peace for those who had lost so much. I believe that all of God's gifts, talents, and anointing are wrapped in a servant's mantle. If you are currently serving others, keep it up! If you are a tired or wounded servant, let God refresh you and heal you. If you have never tried on the servant's mantle, give it a go. You will be blessed!

CHAPTER 58

Trusted Stewards

When we arrived just four or five days earlier, this Mississippi Gulf Coast highway had been littered with cars, boats, parts of houses and trash from the Katrina storm surge. Our intervention team had a very productive time of ministry there and had packed up and headed back to South Carolina. To our surprise, the previously boarded-up Waffle House was open for business! It took several booths to seat all of us, and we all enjoyed our Waffle House favorites.

Recognizing us as disaster responders, the waitress with tears told us her story of survival and the loss of everything she had. Several among us prayed with her, and unbeknownst to one another, gave her a $150 tip! No, it wasn't our money, but it was our money to give. Others back home who could not make the trip themselves had trusted us with cash "to bless someone with or to buy something that's needed."

People who can be trusted with another person's money, children or spouse are "trusted stewards." The Bible is full of examples of trusted stewards. Many a servant has kept the confidence of those around them and maintained a life of integrity and credibility.

Follow That Dream

A trusted steward is not an office to hold, but rather a witness to a commitment to God and His ways. The life of Joseph (Genesis chapters 37, 39 and following) is one of the most complete stories of a trusted servant. It is much easier to build and maintain trust than it is to regain it once it is lost. We all know the tragic stories of those who were once trusted, but yielded to the lure of money, sex or heresy. Somehow, they became too important to need accountability.

Everyone needs to build accountability into their lives, marriage, business and ministry. It is best that accountability be requested or built in instead of imposed. Things like pride will keep us independent instead of interdependent. People who avoid or resist accountability are easy targets for the devil. Like a tactical team movement, we need those trusted friends with us watching over our blind spots. Personal accountability is one of the major reasons for our longevity in marriage and ministry.

Loyalty to a person or group includes humbly telling them what they don't want to hear so as to spare them a lot of pain and sorrow. I do hope you value personal stewardship and accountability. "For a bishop must be blameless, as the steward of God; not self willed, not soon angry, not given to wine, no striker, not given to filthy lucre; But a lover of hospitality, a lover of good men, sober, just, holy, temperate; Holding fast the faithful word as he hath been taught, that he may be able by sound doctrine both to exhort and to convince the gainsayers" (Titus 1:7-9).

CHAPTER 59

Yellow Ribbons

Both sides of Freedom Highway were lined with trees full of yellow ribbons. That was Camp Lajune, North Carolina, over twenty years ago. Our two oldest grandchildren were born there while their father was in the Corp. His firstborn, our only grandson, was born during Desert Shield. Wes was around five months old before his dad had the chance to see him. The yellow ribbons spoke loud and clear of the change of the American spirit concerning the return of her troops since the time our fighting men and women returned from Vietnam. It was like seeing the beginning of a new birth of appreciation for those serving in our military. There was a new sense of pride. The words "duty" and "honor" were being returned to our vocabulary. No longer did we see the scourge of indifference and hatred that met our returning troops from Vietnam. Freedom Highway had awakened that new sense of pride in me, and I witnessed it again in full force just after the 9/11 terrorist attacks.

While responding to Ground Zero in New York City, my partner and I passed under bridges over I-95 that were decorated with American flags and banners proclaiming, "God Bless America." A few of those bridges were occupied by small cheering crowds of flag wavers. Wow! Terrorists had thought they would bring America to her knees, but their attacks actually brought her to her feet!

Follow That Dream

Many talk about freedom and even demand it, but freedom is bought with a price. History, especially American history, clearly depicts that it is the young and courageous that defend our shores. I saw firsthand the results of the Ground Zero attack and the resolve of those who responded. I personally escorted loved ones of those who lost their lives at World Trade to the family observation points. I was honored to quietly stand with them as they tried to deal with their loss at the very site of their loved ones' death. I spent hours on duty with first responders at the dig, at their staging areas and their precincts. In the jaws of adversity and carnage, without tiring, they did their duty.

Those who stand against our foes and defend our liberty do so with life and limb. Their families suffer great losses along with them. We who remain at home must pray without ceasing for them, thank God for those who defend our freedom, and keep tying those yellow ribbons. You don't hear many sermons these days on duty, but duty is a part of our Lord's discourse.

"The apostles said to the Lord, 'Show us how to increase our faith.' The Lord answered, 'If you had faith even as small as a mustard seed, you could say to this mulberry tree, "May you be uprooted and thrown into the sea," and it would obey you! When a servant comes in from plowing or taking care of sheep, does his master say, "Come in and eat with me?" No, he says, "Prepare my meal, put on your apron, and serve me while I eat. Then you can eat later." And does the master thank the servant for doing what he was told to do? Of course not. In the same way, when you obey me you should say, "We are unworthy servants who have simply done our duty"'" (Luke 17:5-10, NLT).

SECTION SEVEN

CHAPTER 60

Back to Her Roots

It had been fifty years since Judy's family moved to the South. I can look out any window and see my roots. I have lived the majority of my life within a seven-mile radius of where I live now. Not so for Judy. So, we planned a trip to retrace her roots. Judy and I drove over 1800 miles to the land of her fathers.

We started our journey in Lancaster County, Pennsylvania for a wonderful Leadership Conference while staying in the lovely home of some new friends. We then traveled several hours west to have lunch with some very dear old friends from Liberty Bible College and Liberty Fellowship. Our paths have crisscrossed many times since the Liberty days, but there is nothing like being in their home for a visit. Then we headed further west to Barnsboro, Pennsylvania where Judy was born. All her aunts and uncles have passed away and her last cousin who lived there just recently moved to live close to her sister.

We arrived when it was just getting dark, so we stopped by the only little motel in town. In was a surprise in many ways. First, I was leery because it was located above a restaurant and bar. While I was checking out the place, Judy began telling the proprietor that she was on a pilgrimage during her year of Jubilee. It turned out that the proprietor's grandmother had lived next door to Judy's grandmother behind the old Mt. Carmel Catholic Church and knew some of the Marino family history. He also told Judy that they used the Mt. Carmel red sauce in their spaghetti receipt. There was no need to check anything else!

The small European style hotel upstairs was excellent, clean and newly remodeled. We tossed our bags in the room and head for the restaurant downstairs to get some of that Marino sauce.

The next morning after breakfast we went to see where Grandmother Marino's house had stood. Now it was a cleared lot right behind the Catholic Church where she attended Mass every morning. Judy spoke of remembering when the entire yard was planted in herbs, vegetables and flowers. We picked some small flowers nestled among the closely cut grass and placed them upon the outline of the old foundation as a gift on an altar. From that place, Judy thanked God for her heritage and her grandmother's love.

We then traveled to the Assemblies of God church that Judy's grandfather helped establish. He was an Irish coal miner. Hearing about the Azusa Street Revival around 1908, he went to tarrying meetings in Pittsburgh and received the Holy Spirit. Returning to Barnsboro, he was very instrumental in establishing that church. I remember Judy's Dad telling me about when their new pastor, David Wilkerson, Sr. came to town with a car full of kids. Judy's father Charley married a Catholic girl, Mary, and the rest is history.

One Couple's Journey

One day when Charley came out of the mines he was met with the comment "Hey Charley, hear about Mary, she got the Holy Ghost!" Her Pentecostal blessing didn't thrill everyone, but time took care of a lot of that. Breaking tradition is not always popular and can be very painful sometimes.

Our next stop on this pilgrimage was Living Waters Campground in Cherry Tree, just a few miles west of Barnsboro. The campgrounds were idle, but the Lord's presence was real. Judy was delighted to show me the place she attended camp meetings as a child. There was a huge tabernacle in the center. The dirt floor that had been covered with sawdust had been upgraded with roughly finished concrete and the wooden benches now had backs on them. The big doors along each side were closed, but it was easy to imagine the crowds of worshippers flowing in and out of the services.

The biggest prize was locating the flowing well (Living Waters) that had been capped. In the middle of the cap was a rusty spigot. After several turns of the handle, the water began to flow. At first it was black and then rusty and then crystal clear. We washed our hands before making that well into another altar, thanking God for the experience of feeling His presence and seeing His healing miracles as a child.

We wondered which one of the little one-room cabins belonged to her aunt's. Most were empty, but one had a single cot, a small dresser, a straight back chair and a small mirror hanging from a nail. Clearly, personal comfort took second place to meeting with God at Living Waters Campground. There by the driveway stood the caretaker's house where Judy's Grandfather and Grandmother Boyle lived after he retired from working in the mines.

Judy was overflowing and ready to turn east towards her second childhood home in New Jersey. We passed by the town where her sister Mary had attended nursing school. We savored the beautiful scenery and the picturesque farms, but mostly we enjoyed talking about her wonderful heritage and the blessing of having her share it with me. After twenty years in the mines, Judy's dad had contracted black lung disease. He had quit school as a young man and entered the mines so that some of his siblings could complete their educations. After a partial lung removal, he moved his family to Merchantville, New Jersey and bought a nursing home, which was our next stop.

Again, we arrived at our destination at dusk. We went straight to the location. It was as Judy had remembered it, except that it was no longer in the superb shape it had been when Charley and Mary owned it. Around the corner was Aunt Charlotte's Candy Store where Judy used to buy small bags of candy as a girl. Around another corner was her girlfriend Cornelia's house.

I wish that Judy could have sat on the porch with Cornelia like they did as children and told her about the trip to Switzerland we took years before. Her elementary school on Center Street is still in operation; the Community Center is still hosting functions.

Then we met up with the highlight of the evening, Mary Kay, Judy's sister in law. We met at a Jersey Diner where the movie Jersey Girl was filmed and had dinner in the booth where the stars had sat. The real stars that night were recollections of relatives and the leading man was Judy's brother Charley. The entire Boyle Family had left Jersey except Charley. He had worked, raised his two sons and died there. After a wonderful night at Mary Kay's home and breakfast at Charley's favorite diner, we set sail for home. We never once turned on the stereo or radio during the entire trip; we just rode and talked. It wasn't quite as spiffy as a Swiss Air flight, but "Thelma Lou," our vintage touring car, was "so fine!"

It was a trip of a lifetime retracing Judy's roots. Finally, I was able to see with my own eyes the places where altars of heritage were built by her godly ancestors.

CHAPTER 61

Parenting is Not for Cowards

When Judy finished reading the book *Parenting is Not for Cowards*, she turned to the back cover and kissed the author's picture!

When we were young believers with young children, *Little House on the Prairie* was the perfect parenting model. If your children didn't toe the line, then the biblical example of Eli and his wayward sons (1 Samuel 1-3) was thrown in your face. God help you if you were a church leader with "rebellious" kids. I'm sure you have heard some variation of the joke concerning whether the preacher's kids or the deacon's kids behaved the worst. In the eyes of many back then, kids were either godly or rebellious. There was no in between.

Judy and I have felt the awful sting of criticism or rebuke that came through a church lay leader or member when our children fell off the Little House wagon. I remember one such encounter with an overseer who felt he should give me correction concerning a situation with one of our children. I'm sure the motive of the message was to help bring restoration, but the attitude and delivery stunk. Judy and I were already at wits' end with the situation. We had disciplined, cried and prayed that God would intervene. One thing we had determined to never put on our children was the burden, "Look what you are doing to me and my ministry." That would be too unfair.

One Couple's Journey

Trust me, there were times when Judy and I discussed giving the house to the kids, driving the car towards Canada until we ran out of gas and then starting to walk. While we surely had our moments, we never fled to Canada. However, we did cry out to God for wisdom and strength. "God is our refuge and strength, a very present help in trouble. Therefore will not we fear, though the earth be removed, and though the mountains be carried into the midst of the sea; Though the waters thereof roar and be troubled, though the mountains shake with the swelling thereof. Selah. There is a river, the streams whereof shall make glad the city of God, the holy place of the tabernacles of the most High. God is in the midst of her; she shall not be moved: God shall help her, and that right early" (Psalms 46:1-5).

Thanks be to God; the Farnum family made it through all those crises. Many a time the Lord sent us unlikely loving allies with wisdom and practical support. We love our children and are proud of them! They are all parents themselves now and the eldest is a grandparent. They are all doing life well and have their own relationship with the Lord.

Atz Kiltar on the T.V. series "Alaska the Last Frontier" recalled a parenting principal passed down from his father, "Teach your children well and love them." The Bible says, "Direct your children onto the right path, and when they are older, they will not leave it" (Proverbs 22:6, NLT). There were also very funny stories along the journey of parenting and pastoring.

One day at church, Judy stopped a young boy at the bottom of the banister, telling him that he should not be sliding down it. To that he replied, "Miss Judy will you please let my Mommy tell me what I should or should not do?"

Another lady at church was having a problem with one of her kids during the Sunday morning service. The disruption intensified as she dragged the kid out the building and around the corner to begin her Sunday morning rebuke. In her huff, she didn't realize they were just beneath a sanctuary window from which everyone inside could hear all that was going on. I didn't have to tell a funny story in the sermon that morning. We had already had a good laugh.

Our kids loved to catch critters. On one outing, they decided to go pet the geese down by the pond. The next thing we heard was yells and screams as they came tearing across the field with several honking, flapping geese in pursuit. The kids also fancied themselves as spies in our neighborhood, thinking no one could see or hear them. The family beach trips were a blast with stories galore. We all remember Fanny's beach house! And later, the Jeep gave them miles and miles of fun and freedom. Who can forget the blue rabbit? And what about the stories that we haven't heard yet like the side trip to Houston? Old stories will emerge from time to time at family gatherings, perhaps even this year when we go to the beach. It is a different house, but we are still making wonderful memories!

"The Lord isn't really being slow about his promise, as some people think. No, he is being patient for your sake. He does not want anyone to be destroyed, but wants everyone to repent" (2 Peter 3:9, NLT).

CHAPTER 62

They Can't Move!

Judy and I looked at each other in utter disbelief. This could not be true. "They can't move!," we said to each other.

We had been praying and believing that they would take over the leadership of the church, not move to Canada as missionaries. Judy and I have long understood that a big part of our ministry is to equip others for the work of ministry, make room for them to serve and give opportunities for them to excel. Several other couples had been in the process of becoming key leaders through the years, but various things kept it from happening. Each time it caused a great setback to the church and very precious momentum was lost. This time we were very confident that Joey and Renee were God's choice.

Though Judy and I never discussed this idea with anyone, including Joey and Renee, we felt that our time at the helm was ending and the church needed to move into a new era with fresh, younger leadership. Now, what seemed to be the Lord's leading and will hit a brick wall. History had repeated itself. They were moving! We asked the Lord, "Why?" He only told us to continue being faithful at Bethel and trust Him.

During this same period, I had read a great book on leadership that contained a life-changing chapter on how we measure success. This author offered a different approach than many. He proclaimed, "The mark of a successful person is that he or she has a successor!" Wow! What a revelation. Someone had not only challenged the old system of measuring success but was insightful enough to give a truer measuring stick. I have watched natural fathers as well as spiritual fathers make their sons wait too long before the reins were handed over. Or, they held on to one of the reins to the frustration of the younger leader. I received a pearl of wisdom recently from a second-generation frontiersman, "Teach your children well and love them. Trust that God can speak to them and trust that they can hear His voice." After all our efforts at parenting, we had to simply trust God!

Years ago at the National Leadership Conference at Ridgecrest, North Carolina, I was privileged to have dinner with an old friend and mentor who invited two of the main speakers for the conference for our dinner meeting. We were dining at a local restaurant after the evening session when the discussion between these three turned to church growth and leadership. One of the high profile speakers really got my attention when he said, "I believe that when a church is twenty-five years old, it should be bulldozed to the ground and a new one should be started in another location. They should not use any of the old bricks in the new building!" The second speaker seconded the notion.

Early in our tenure, a powerful prophecy came forth concerning Bethel. The proven prophet declared, "Hold not my disciples once they are strengthened, for though this church be a small church, it shall be a strong church!" That has been our history. For the most part, those whom we have discipled and readied for leadership, God moved on to other places.

Well, here we were at Bethel, about twenty-five years old, everything paid for, everything smooth. With all these thoughts going around and around in my head, Judy and I knew we had to wait on the Lord's timing. We have witnessed firsthand the destruction that followed when a tired leader held on to the reins too long or threw them to the wrong person out of desperation. So, we continued to quietly believe in God's faithfulness. "O Jacob, how can you say the Lord does not see your troubles? O Israel, how can you say God ignores your rights? Have you never heard? Have you never understood? The Lord is the everlasting God, the Creator of all the earth. He never grows weak or weary. No one can measure the depths of his understanding. He gives power to the weak and strength to the powerless. Even youths will become weak and tired, and young men will fall in exhaustion. But those who trust in the Lord will find new strength. They will soar high on wings like eagles. They will run and not grow weary. They will walk and not faint" (Isaiah 40:27-31, NLT).

CHAPTER 63

The Phone Rang

About two years had gone by since Joey and Renee moved to Canada. One day out of the blue, the phone rang. It was Joey. After a few minutes of getting caught up, Joey said, "The Lord has been speaking to us about returning to Bethel."

Wow! Come On! Joey had been apart of Bethel since a teenager. After attending Liberty Bible College, he and Renee married and became an awesome team for the Lord. They had begun their ministry together here at Bethel and after seeing the world outside of Orangeburg, the Lord was leading their return. Our successors were chosen and would be arriving as soon as they could turn over their ministry obligations in Canada.

The Lord had orchestrated the choice of successors and we determined to let Him direct the transition also. Being the founding pastor with a twenty-seven year tenure can be tough on your replacement. Judy and I begin to prepare the transition. Several principles came into play that are foundational for a win/win transition. These principles determine the emotional and spiritual stability of the church.

First, the reputation of the predecessor dictates the rights and limitations of the new leadership. Since there were no real issues dictating our retirement, Joey and Renee didn't have a lot of negatives to overcome.

Secondly, Joey and Renee already knew how to honor those who have gone before you.

Thirdly, we gave them the reins as soon as the congregation accepted our retirement and could see for themselves that this was the will of God. It was a God thing!

Folks occasionally ask, "Are you still the pastor of Bethel?"

We answer, "No, Judy and I turned it over to a younger couple five years ago and they are doing great!"

"Well, where do you attend now?" is usually the next question.

"We're still at Bethel. Joey is my pastor and I sit on the back row and play with the grand babies!"

Actually, we do serve on the leadership team and help Joey train new leaders or assist in any way that will be a support to him and Renee. I know it's not the norm, but God has allowed us to do church differently. God has blessed this attitude, and we have a success story instead of a the type of horror stories that we have heard all too many times.

Years ago, I was confronted by a very influential member of the church and given that last-ditch ultimatum concerning a God-sent couple in our church leadership. "Either they go, or I go!" I assure you, the Lord helped me with that one because Farnums don't usually handle ultimatums like that very pleasantly.

"You know, this is not my church nor your church, this is the Lord's church. I wonder who the Lord would tell that they are not welcome here anymore?"

The influential "I, my, me" decided to leave instead of bending the knee to the lordship of Jesus Christ.

We must not ever forget that we are members, stewards, not owners of the Lord's church! "Submitting yourselves one to another in the fear of God. Wives, submit yourselves unto your own husbands, as unto the Lord. For the husband is the head of the wife, even as Christ is the head of the church: and he is the savior of the body. Therefore as the church is subject unto Christ, so let the wives be to their own husbands in every thing. Husbands, love your wives, even as Christ also loved the church, and gave himself for it; That he might sanctify and cleanse it with the washing of water by the word, That he might present it to himself a glorious church, not having spot, or wrinkle, or any such thing; but that it should be holy and without blemish. So ought men to love their wives as their own bodies. He that loveth his wife loveth himself. For no man ever yet hated his own flesh; but nourisheth and cherisheth it, even as the Lord the church: For we are members of his body, of his flesh, and of his bones. For this cause shall a man leave his father and mother, and shall be joined unto his wife, and they two shall be one flesh. This is a great mystery: but I speak concerning Christ and the church" (Ephesians 5:21-32).

CHAPTER 64

Another Closed Chapter

Judy and I just closed another chapter in our journey. After seventeen years as a law enforcement chaplain serving in the Sheriff's Office, the door has closed again. I was the most prepared than I have ever been. Judy had returned to work after her brain surgery four years earlier while the Sheriff's Office was in a lot of turmoil.

Out of that upheaval arose a new Sheriff that we thought we knew, but it wasn't long before we started seeing and hearing things that really concerned us. Over a period of about a year the Sheriff became distant and his agenda slowly changed. I believe the Lord put it in my heart that I would not contend with another sheriff. At his first opportunity, I was terminated. Judy remained for about six months in her office just two doors down the hall from the Sheriff. She and I filled out our retirement papers one Sunday night, and the rest is history.

I have been on a sabbatical for the past year. I always wondered how ministers continued to have income while on extended sabbaticals and now I know. Most of last year I worked concrete construction. Currently I am helping a young man re-establish his tree and land service business and I volunteer at a small police department in our county. My current work schedule doesn't allow me to respond to crises very often, but I'm at peace with that. I know God is aware of all this, so I am resting in Him until the next assignment.

CHAPTER 65

Miraculous Mud

For the second time in my life, I should have died, but God spared my life again. The first time was in 1969 when I was in the Naval shipwreck described earlier. This time in 2015 it was a tractor accident. We were preparing a retention pond for hydro seeding. I was operating a small tractor on top of the dam which was pulling a harrow along the dam's slope. I turned my head briefly to check the harrow's position and inadvertently pulled the steering wheel toward the inside slope. It only took a moment, and the tractor began to roll sideways down the embankment. I thought I was clear, but as soon as I hit the bottom of the dry pond, the rear tire slammed into my back and legs. The weight of the tractor mashed me into the muddy bottom face first. Because of the pressure against my back and rib cage, I could only catch shallow breaths. I wiggled my toes and moved my feet, checking to see if my back was broken.

Five guys who were working with a different company in the vicinity heard the crash and looked around the fence corner. They saw me pinned under the rear tire with the tractor turned up on its side. They ran to the scene. I told them I could not breathe and asked if they could please try to relieve some of the pressure from my back. They were able to give me enough help that I could take two deep breaths. One of the guys ran for a nearby excavator and used it to lift the tractor off me while the other four pulled me to safety.

Despite their protest, I stood up amongst them looking like some kind of a swamp monster. I had mud plastered from head to toe. I walked with their assistance to the top of the dam and then walked towards the ambulance that had arrived. I knew who I was and what day it was as they checked my blood pressure. My pain level was low because I was still numb from the impact, but I did admit to some soreness. I reported a large hematoma on my right thigh with tire tread imprints on either side. The EMTs gave me all kinds of reasons why I needed to go to the emergency room, but I opted out.

At home, I was greeted by my youngest daughter Grace and her five-year-old daughter Maddy. There I stood in the kitchen with chunks of mud falling off me when Judy walked in. "Honey, I don't think I can bend over, so if you will take my boots off, I'll tell you what happened." We rejoiced together that the Lord had saved me from serious injury or death, after which I gingerly stood up and walked out on the patio, stripped off all those muddy clothes and went back inside for a shower.

I do a lot of physical work, so I knew that whatever position I chose next was the one I would be in for some time. It was all comfy clothes, Ibuprofen and my 10-year-old unused recliner for the next several days. I thought I would break in half at any moment, especially when I occasionally coughed from the previous week's cold.

After two weeks of being completely stoved-up, I returned to work on limited duty. I noticed some improvement every day. Three weeks after the accident, I had my first scheduled appointment with my new doctor. She listened to my story, poked my hematoma, which was smaller by this time, and listened to my breathing while pushing against my ribs. When all that was done, she said, "You're a miracle!"

Well, I thank God for His mercy. I had no fear while under that tractor. I did speak the name of Jesus and I told Judy that I loved her. While we were waiting on the ambulance, I told my rescuers, "The one thing I have learned from my shipwreck in 1969 and from this accident this afternoon is that a man needs to be ready to die at any moment because at any moment he could!" Talk about a captured audience!

The Bible says, "People die once, and after that they are judged. Likewise, Christ was sacrificed once to take away the sins of humanity, and after that he will appear a second time. This time he will not deal with sin, but he will save those who eagerly wait for him" (Hebrews 9:27-28, GW). I did not fear death because I have a Savior! There is nothing else on this earth what is more fulfilling than being born of the Spirit and walking with Jesus. He alone can lead us into the abundant life. We become better at every aspect of life as we walk in the anointing of our purpose, our destiny.

One Couple's Journey

I was first introduced to this concept early in my Christian walk. Anointed men and women of God taught me the principles of walking with Jesus. I began to see His promises working in my life and the lives of others. I began to trust Him and respond to His voice. He taught me to be a better husband, better father and better friend. He gave me a life of service, filled with adventure and reward, the best of which is to see Him move in the life of others, knowing that He chose you to be a part of the process in some small way.

This same Jesus has a plan for your life that is better than the best plan you have. Why not begin trusting Him today? It's the best life ever!

CHAPTER 66

One More Mountain

"One more mountain" is what I heard in my spirit. As a boy, "Butchie's Adventures" were mostly imaginary. They became more real as I grew older and was met with more words of caution from others. Now at sixty-seven all the talk is about retirement and the complaint that "you can't do what you use to do." Well, my body has clearly defined to me my current limitations, but my spirit man still yearns for adventure and there is plenty to be had. I am sure more sermons have been preached about the failings of the children of Israel during the journey to the promised land than about the exploits of Caleb and Joshua, who were on the same journey, being led by the same leader, under the same circumstances. The difference was that they had a different spirit! I can relate very well to the definition that John Wayne gave for courage. "Courage is being scared to death—but saddling up anyway."

I am not any of the afore-mentioned heroes, but you don't have to be a hero to conquer mountains! My mountains have been both internal and external. I have been privileged to work among men and women of a different spirit most of my adult life. I would characterize them as "those who run toward what everyone else is running away from!"

The first responders of 911 are prime examples. Fear of giants and such will keep us in the safety zone as a spectator. I look back on one particular commanding officer that I served under during my three tours in Vietnam. He always got us out front and stretched men and machine beyond the norm. His appearance surely didn't fit the "macho man" profile, but inside, he was a mountain taker. He had a different spirit and his example challenged me to the core.

Many have been inspired and have plenty of information, but it takes a different spirit to conquer mountains. I'm not sure what the formula is for a different spirit, but I do know that fear is the natural enemy of courage. It must be set aside and overcome. This happens by the word of the Lord.

During the late 80s I was challenged by John Maxwell as he taught on Principles of Leadership and other strategies of mountain taking. I watched with amazement one day as John dropped his ice cream cone at the lunch table. He was making a gesture with his cone-filled hand and there it went. Plop! The ice cream had no sooner hit the floor than three or more guys jumped to their feet to get him another cone! They wanted to be close to him because he inspired them! I often came back from such conferences and shared what I had excited me. Many were excited with me and were ready for the charge. Others ran the information through their paradigm filter and said things like, "Well now, we have to be careful..." I will be responsible, but please do not ask me to be careful!

I appreciate the years of being a support member of our agency's SWAT team. Though my place as Chaplain was on the sideline, they would always ask me during training if I wanted to take a turn also. "Yes" I would reply.

A few years ago, Judy and I gave each of our children a recent picture of me repelling down a tower during a SWAT in-service training. Attached to the picture frame was a short length of braided cord, with the exclamation "When you get to the end of your rope, tie a knot in it and hold on!" That's what I'm doing today, holding on. I am standing, as described in Ephesians 6:13-14, until God shows me the next mountain. I plan to give it another go. It's in my spirit and I'm excited! "Now therefore give me this mountain, whereof the Lord spake in that day; for thou heardest in that day how the Anakims were there, and that the cities were great and fenced: if so be the Lord will be with me, then I shall be able to drive them out, as the Lord said. And Joshua blessed him, and gave unto Caleb the son of Jephunneh Hebron for an inheritance" (Joshua 14:12-13).

What has the Lord spoken to your spirit?

CHAPTER 67

Prophetic Promise

It was an exciting day when Judy and I became great-grandparents! We thought we would be at least one hundred and ten years old before having great grandchildren, but He worked it out while we were in our late sixties. Several days after Hunter's birth, the Lord dropped a word in my heart concerning Hunter. The Lord said, "There is greatness within him. The nations will know his name."

For days before we would travel to see our newest son in the family, I pondered the promise of God. After checking all his fingers and toes, I spoke those words over him as I held him in my arms. This was a special God moment for me because both of my grandfathers died before I was born. I am thankful that God spared my life time and again so I could continue to speak that word over him. What a joy! "Children's children are the crown of old men; and the glory of children are their fathers" (Proverbs 17:6).

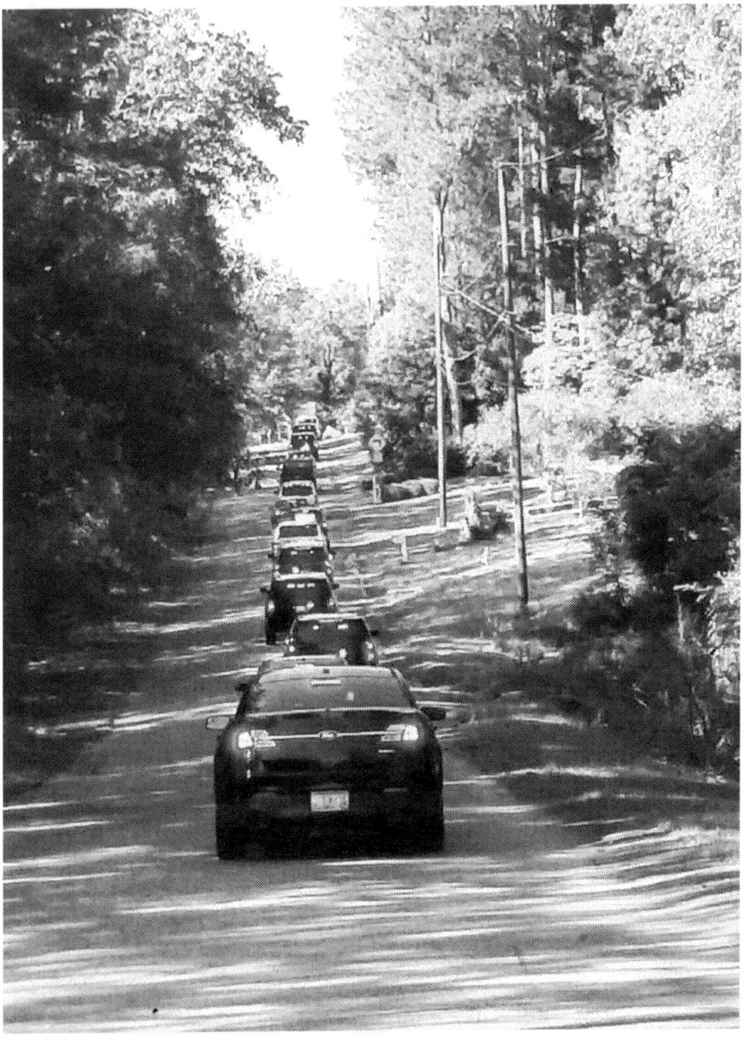

CHAPTER 68

A Fitting Tribute to "Momma Judy"

It was Friday afternoon and some forty patrol vehicles from two counties paraded down our street in honor of "Momma Judy." Judy had died the day before. As the cars passed in review with lights and sirens, her five children waved and cheered their passing. Each deputy showed their love and respect for the lady who had somehow touched their lives with God's love and grace.

Also fitting was the rainbow that was captured in several photos as it rested above the patrol cars in front of our house. Our children said, "Look, look at the rainbow!" Judy had a lifelong love for rainbows.

On the previous Tuesday we had moved Judy into a front bedroom with a hospital bed so we could attend to her better. On Wednesday, Judy and I had a great day together. She ate a good breakfast of grits and eggs and enjoyed the view of our front yard from one of her favorite rooms. After her dinner, she went to sleep quickly and rested peacefully. I was awakened twice during the night by her coughing, but when I checked on her, she was sleeping peacefully.

When I entered her room at 6:30 the next morning to start her morning routine of a warm washcloth for her face, brushing her hair and a cup of hot coffee, things had drastically changed. Her breathing was labored and there was that unmistakable rattle in her chest. The children gathered and after a telephone visit with our doctor, hospice was called in. After a brief evaluation, the hospice nurse told us that Judy was in transition and had only perhaps hours or minutes to live. Oxygen was given to help her breathing and the children took over the care of their mother.

That was a healing time for our family. Each of us can get terribly busy with life as we know it, and so much is taken for granted. The focus that day was Judy and her hands-on care. During the afternoon and night, her children and I spent time with her individually and as a group. We prayed, we cried, and we laughed together. Shortly after midnight, Judy broke free from this earthly body and went to her heavenly home to be with her Lord.

EPILOGUE

I have tried to tell the story of our fifty-three years together, but Judy's story can best be told by the hundreds of people that encountered her. The one thing that we absolutely agreed on was that we were going to follow Jesus no matter where He led us! Beyond that, Judy was Judy and Butch was Butch!

I would advise anyone who has decided to abandon their life to follow Jesus to do just that. He is not our co-pilot; He is the pilot. We don't have the strength within ourselves to live the life or follow the dream He has given us. Judy loved Jesus and she devoured His Word. She was not a preacher nor a musician nor a worship leader. Judy was a handmaiden who worshiped her Lord and met people with His compassion and grace. Her life and love attracted the downtrodden and the unaccepted. She was Judy. I loved her just the way she was and together, we followed that dream!

What a life, what a love, what a treasured adventure! Judy had finished her race well. Now I am waiting for my next mountain to be revealed, holding Judy close in my heart!

Made in the USA
Columbia, SC
12 September 2024